THE SWANAGE BRANCH

Contents

Front Cover:
With branch Driver Jack Spicer at the far end of the 'push-pull' train, Fireman Keith Sloper is at the controls of Victorian-designed 'M7' 0-4-4T No 30108 as she simmers patiently at Corfe Castle's down platform, whilst working the 15.15 Wareham to Swanage train on Sunday 7 July 1963. *C. L. Caddy*

Back Cover (top):
On the warm early summer evening of Sunday 28 July 1963, Corfe Castle station echoes to the sound of Drummond 'M7' 0-4-4T No 30056, as she eases her two-coach Maunsell push-pull set away from the down platform with the 16.45 Wareham to Swanage train. Corfe signalman cycles along the platform after exchanging the key token for the tablet. *Rae Montgomery*

Back Cover (bottom):
A panoramic view of Swanage station and yard with the town behind, from the Northbrook bridge. With rakes of main line carriages packing the yard, Driver Jack Spicer picks up the pouched Tyer's No 6 Tablet from Swanage Signalman Arthur Galton as 'M7' No 30108 'Rosie' accelerates past the LSWR signalbox with the 15.58 to Corfe Castle and Wareham on the afternoon of Sunday 7 July 1963. *C. L. Caddy*

First published 1987
Third edition published 1993

ISBN 0 7110 2189 9

All rights reserved. No part of this book may be reproduced or transmitted in any form or by any means, electronic or mechanical, including photocopying, recording or by any information storage and retrieval system, without permission from the Publisher in writing.

© Ian Allan Ltd 1993

Published by Ian Allan Ltd, Shepperton, Surrey; and printed by Ian Allan Printing Ltd at their works at Coombelands in Runnymede, England.

Acknowledgements

I should like to thank the many friends who have helped me, especially Peter Frost, Robert Richards and Tony Trood, as well as Roger Aldous, Richard Amott, Ken Andrews, Christopher Ashby, Hugh Ballantyne, Maurice Barnaby, Ted Benn, Edward Bird, John Bird, Arthur Blick, Roger Bray; Kate Brennan and Michaela Horsfield of the *Bournemouth Evening Echo* and its Editor, Mr W. M. Hill; British Petroleum; Colin Caddy, W. A. Camwell, Henry Casserley, John Coleman, Ruth Colyer, John Coogan, the late Derek Cross, Steve Dadd, Peter Downer, Tim Edmonds, D. J. Ehlert, Barry England; English China Clays; Mike Esau, Charles Firminger, J. C. Flemons, David Ford, Lawrence Golden, Arthur Grant; Grant-Lyon Eagre Ltd; Bryan Green, Richard Green, Derek Harrison, Les Hayward, William Hazell, N. J. Hill, James Hunt, Bob Inman, Tony Jervis, Bryan Kimber, Brian Kohring, Chris Legg, Tony Legg, Lens of Sutton, Rodney Lissenden, Colin J. Marsden, Rae Montgomery, George Moon, Reg Moors, David Morgan, Mrs Monnie Moss, Bob and Nona Noble, Fred Norman, the late Charles Orchard, Bryan Owen-Jones; Mrs Lorna Pascall of the Wareham Museum; Ivo Peters, Chris Phillips, Leslie Phillips, Ray Phillips, Lawrence Popplewell, W. Philip Conolly, Robert Prance, D. Trevor Rowe, Alan Saunders, John Scrace, John Sharland, David M. Smith, the Rev Gerald Squarey, Graham Stacey, Alan Thorpe, Martyn Thresh, John M. Tolson, A. B. Tompkins, Peter Treloar, Mrs A. L. Walden, Michael Walshaw, Maurice Walton, Fraser White, Walter 'Chalkie' White, Alan Wild, Don Wright, P. J. M. Wright and Raymund Wright. I should also like to thank the Southern Electric Group, the Branch Line Society and the Locomotive Club of Great Britain for their help.

THE SWANAGE BRANCH

Introduction

This is the complete, bitter-sweet story of the Swanage branch — a 10-mile stretch of single line that ran through the Isle of Purbeck, one of Dorset's most spectacular regions and a protected area of outstanding natural beauty.

A peninsula rather than an island, the Isle is located in the south of the county and flanked by the English Channel to the south and east, Thomas Hardy's moody and brooding heathlands to the west with Poole Harbour and the sprawling Bournemouth-Poole conurbation to the north.

The advent of the entrepreneur-led railway in 1885 was to be expected with Purbeck's expansion and growth in particular, and that of Swanage as a family seaside resort emerging from a quarrying and fishing community in particular. The Isle of Purbeck has always been a bottleneck for traffic; this ever-increasing burden being eased by the branch railway, only for the much-loved line to be closed when the area and its people needed it most with the private car explosion of the 1960s and 1970s.

Although only 10 miles in length, the Swanage branch passed through a constantly changing landscape thanks to Purbeck's multifarious geological structure.

On its way from the ancient Saxon market town of Wareham on the London-Weymouth main line, through the Medieval stone-roofed village of Corfe Castle to the seaside resort of Swanage, the branch passed over lush water meadows; across wild, choking heathland and through the gaunt chalk gap of the Purbeck Hills at Corfe. From here trains wound their way across rough, wind-swept common land, through verdant clay valleys and dense woodland past the famous Purbeck stone quarries of Langton Matravers before arriving in genteel Swanage — just yards from the lapping waters of the bay.

The Isle of Purbeck's many landscapes are magical at any time of year, the addition of an intimate branch railway line irresistible. It was this unique combination that was so fascinating and attracted both passengers and enthusiasts alike in considerable numbers. One distinctive route of the Swanage branch was its sinuous route, swinging left and then right through the Isle — scarcely did the train negotiate one bend before the track ahead disappeared round another. The long London and excursion trains from other parts of the country seemed to snake incessantly on their way down to Corfe Castle and Swanage.

For the overwhelming majority of Purbeck people, 1972 was undoubtedly the end of the Swanage branch. Its apparent death came on the dark night of New Year's Day — the gruesome death throes unmercifully prolonged, the agony lingering for more than half a decade; from the ebullient 1960s to the harsh economic realities of the 1970s.

However, the Swanage branch's death was illusory — its life did not end with the final train, the official closure or even the lifting of the rusty tracks, as with so many of Dorset's vanished and mourned railways — the Somerset & Dorset line from Bournemouth to Bath and the 'Old Road' from Poole to Wimborne and Ringwood immediately coming to mind. In the case of Purbeck's branch line, its people have been given another chance; their railway has not disappeared, its land will not be sold off for a fast buck with the route of the trackbed lost forever.

The memories of the 1960s and early 1970s are being swept away as the Swanage Railway is rebuilt and resuscitated to help solve the Isle of Purbeck's horrendous traffic congestion problems, provide a valuable all-year community rail service and important element in the area's tourism strategy. It is an incredible heart-warming story - and this is it.

Andrew P.M. Wright,
Wareham,
Dorset.
New Year's Day, 1993.

Left:
During her brief holiday in Dorset, Standard 2-6-2T No 82027 was photographed hauling a train to Swanage under Holme Lane on Monday 18 May 1964. In the distance, the line dips to cross the River Frome before climbing up to Worgret Junction. The first concrete sleepers to be used on the branch were laid through Holme in 1953. No 82027 worked the branch between January and October 1964. She was scrapped in April 1966.
Rodney A. Lissenden

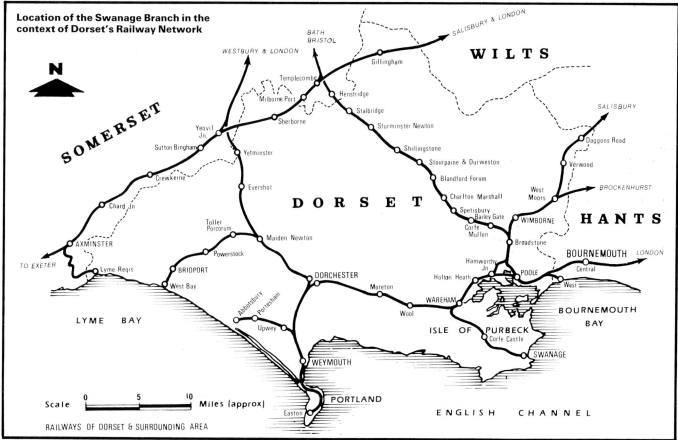

Location of the Swanage Branch in the context of Dorset's Railway Network

N

SOMERSET

WESTBURY & LONDON

BATH BRISTOL

SALISBURY & LONDON

WILTS

Gillingham

Templecombe

Milborne Port

Henstridge

Stalbridge

Sherborne

Sturminster Newton

Yeovil Jn

Sutton Bingham

Yetminster

Shillingstone

SALISBURY

Daggons Road

Crewkerne

Evershot

DORSET

Stourpaine & Durweston

Blandford Forum

Verwood

BROCKENHURST

Chard Jn

Toller Porcorum

Charlton Marshall

West Moors

HANTS

AXMINSTER

Maiden Newton

Powerstock

Spetisbury
Bailey Gate

WIMBORNE

TO EXETER

Lyme Regis

BRIDPORT

Corfe Mullen

Broadstone

BOURNEMOUTH

LONDON

West Bay

DORCHESTER

Hamworthy Jn

POOLE

Central

Moreton

Holton Heath

West

LYME BAY

Abbotsbury
Portesham

Wool

WAREHAM

BOURNEMOUTH BAY

Upwey

ISLE OF PURBECK

Corfe Castle

SWANAGE

WEYMOUTH

Scale 0   5   10 Miles (approx)

PORTLAND

Easton

ENGLISH CHANNEL

RAILWAYS OF DORSET & SURROUNDING AREA

Top:
On a hot summer's day in 1963, 'M7' No 30107 pilots rebuilt 'West Country' Pacific No 34093 *Saunton* on a Swanage-Waterloo train along the Dunshay valley past Woodyhyde and Afflington Farm en route for Corfe Castle. Beyond the curving rake of Bulleid coaches are the woods of Dunshay Manor. No 34093 is passing over bridge No 21 which provided access for Woodyhyde Farm to its land south of the railway. *Mike Esau*

Right:
'Push-pull' fitted Class 33 No D6513 passes the now infamous Creech Bottom crossing on Tuesday 23 March 1971, whilst on her way light engine to collect ball clay from the works of English China Clays at Furzebrook Sidings. Just 11 months later Creech Bottom was the location for a threatened hold-up by the cowboys of the Lazy C. Ranch of the last train to Corfe Castle and Swanage.
Anthony E. Trood

THE SWANAGE BRANCH

1   A trip down the Swanage branch in the summer of 1963

Let us go back over 20 years for our journey down the meandering Swanage branch in the age of steam. The year is 1963 and the day a glorious summer Saturday in early July. Six months previously the branch had been struggling amidst the ice and snow of one of Britain's worst winters of the century, with Dorset's other communications being completely immobilised. Less than four months before, the Beeching Report on the state of the railways had been published; the late Harold Macmillan was Prime Minister, the Profumo affair had broken out the previous month and the shock assassination of President Kennedy was still some four months away.

On this sunny morning Wareham station is a hive of activity; we walk across to the booking hall. The forecourt is full of cars — two Ford Anglias, two Consuls, a Hillman Minx, two Humber Sceptres, a Riley and an Austin Cambridge. Across the way, on the other side of the main road and opposite the station's 1928 signalbox, is the Railway Hotel complete with its marvellous likeness of an SR 'King Arthur'

4-6-0 in tiles above the entrance. We pass from the brightness of the forecourt into the cool shade of the booking hall with its pervasive smell of floor polish, to buy our four-shilling return tickets to Swanage. With a cheery word from the Clerk, Les Hurst, we pass on to the down platform. Looking to the right we can see the soot-covered footbridge with the level crossing and signalbox beyond. Opposite, on the up main, a long line of green Bulleid coaches stand with the magnificent form of a dirty 'Merchant Navy' Pacific at their head. On her tender, a nimble fireman is watering her up before swinging the bag away and climbing down. Meanwhile, on the footplate, her driver casts a discerning eye on the steam chest and boiler pressure gauges. The up starting signal under the footbridge jerks upwards showing a clear road ahead to Holton Heath.

As the Bulleid steadily accelerates away, we turn to the left and walk towards the down bay — platform 1; the little branch train to Swanage comes into view, waiting contentedly. At the rear of the two coaches and against the stopblocks 'M7' class

No 30108 (affectionately known as 'Rosie' to the crews) simmers quietly whilst her Driver, Jack Spicer, and Fireman, Keith Sloper, have a chat with the Guard, Alec Dudley. A seat is found in one of the immaculate Maunsell coaches — the pride of Bournemouth West's carriage cleaning team. To the chatter of excited holidaymakers, a down stopping train from Waterloo and Bournemouth comes to a halt outside the window. At the head is rebuilt Bulleid Pacific No 35022 *Holland America Line* with steam leaking from every orifice; with a shrill whistle our train moves off. We pass the water crane and cross on to the main line. No 30108 puffs with determination and our train accelerates up the gradient heading for Worgret

Below left:
The grand exterior of Wareham station on Sunday 15 December 1968, looking across the forecourt. The station was formally opened at 7.00am on Monday 4 April 1887, replacing the original 1847 station on the Bournemouth side of the footbridge. Curiously, unlike Corfe Castle and Swanage stations which were built in 1884, Wareham's 1886 station is a listed building. *Tony M. Jervis*

Above right:
Branch and main trains at Wareham. The crew of Ivatt tank No 41303 at the south bay platform 1 wait to haul the next train to Corfe Castle and Swanage on Saturday 4 July 1964, whilst GWR 'Hall' No 4920 waits at platform 2 with a Bournemouth-Weymouth train. Behind No 41303 are the main station buildings. *Anthony E. Trood*

Right:
On the fine morning of Sunday 2 July 1967, with less than eight days of Southern steam remaining, 3-coach 'Tadpole' DEMU No 1201 idles at Wareham's up main platform after arriving with the branch train from Swanage. With the impending implementation of full main line diesel traction between Bournemouth and Weymouth, Wareham's stripped platform canopies completed BR's new 'clean' image. *Anthony E. Trood*

Junction and the start of the Swanage branch. Through the window, on the opposite side of the carriage, the old Wareham walls can be discerned behind the plumes of passing smoke and steam.

Approaching Worgret Junction, the train passes under the A352 Wareham to Wool main road bridge before swinging left on to the single branch track. With 'Rosie' slowing to a mere 10mph, her driver leans from the Maunsell's driving cab to collect the pouch containing the Key-Token for the section to Corfe Castle from Signalman Arthur Blick. After rounding the curve in the cutting, our train accelerates; the line falls to the viaduct over the River Frome and then we take the long climb up through the woods of Holme and over the Grange Road that leads to Creech. On the right, beyond the hamlet of Creech, can be seen the backbone of Purbeck, the massive Purbeck Hills, with — like a herculean cist — the ancient Creech Barrow, the site of Iron Age burials. Clattering over the Creech Bottom crossing, where the last branch train would almost be held up nine years later, our train — the 11.30 from Wareham — heads up the final straight to Furzebrook and the branch's first summit.

We cross the tumuli-ridden heath: it is a long climb, which comes to an end as the train sweeps under a brick road bridge and

Left:
After arriving from Swanage, Standard '4' 2-6-4T No 80147 runs round her two Maunsell coaches at Wareham on Thursday 30 July 1964. Leaning from the cab is Driver Jock Hapgood. Behind No 80147 is the station footbridge with, beyond, the main road level crossing, signalbox and goods yard. No 80147 first worked to Swanage in August 1963 with the last occasion being June 1965, just before she was withdrawn from Bournemouth MPD. *Anthony E. Trood*

Below left:
The branch train for Swanage as many travellers remember it. On a hot summer Sunday in 1962, 'M7' 0-4-4T No 30379 simmers with her Maunsell 'push-pull' set at Wareham's south bay platform 1, waiting for her next departure to Corfe and Swanage. The main Bournemouth to Weymouth line is to the right, whilst to the left is the station water tower, sadly demolished in June 1972. No 30379 was built in 1904 at Nine Elms and withdrawn from Three Bridges in October 1963; she was cut up at Eastleigh. *Anthony E. Trood*

Above right:
After leaving Wareham, branch trains ran along the main line for 1¼ miles, climbing at a gradient of 1 in 200 up to Worgret Junction. Here, on Sunday 4 July 1965, Standard '4' 2-6-0 No 76011 is tackling the

climb with her eight-coach 09.45 Eastleigh to Swanage train after crossing the River Piddle and passing Wareham Common.
    Behind the train in the distance is Northport and the tall chimney of the old Sandford brickworks, demolished in 1980. *Anthony E. Trood*

Below:
Route of the Swanage branch line through the Isle of Purbeck.

passes Furzebrook Sidings. In the loop is Standard '4' 2-6-0 No 76026, her mixed traffic lining and totem scarcely discernible beneath the grime. She simmers patiently with a rake of empty ball clay wagons, waiting for us to pass out of the section before she can exchange them for full wagons from Pike Brothers Fayle & Co's siding. 'Rosie' steadily accelerates over another girder bridge under which used to

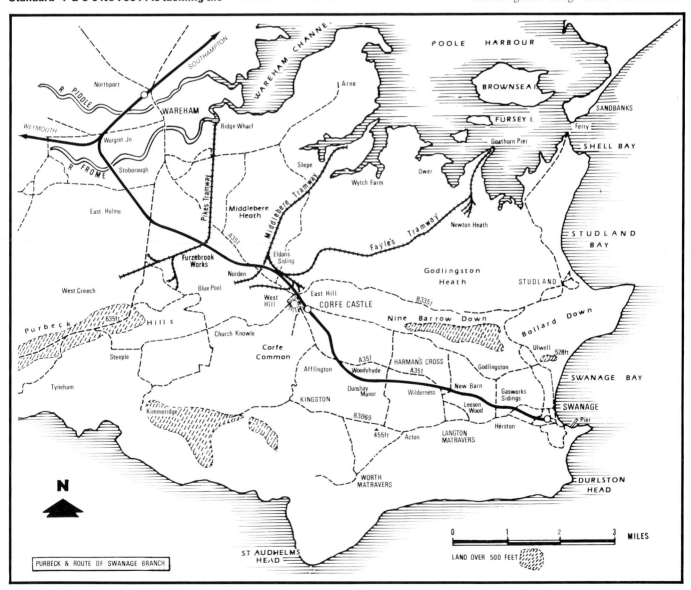

Left:
Worgret Junction on Saturday 25 July 1964. Rebuilt 'Battle of Britain' Bulleid Pacific No 34085 *501 Squadron* leads her long Swanage to Waterloo train past the signalbox and off the branch before descending into Wareham. Behind the signalbox, closed on Sunday 23 May 1976, and demolished on Monday 16 January 1978, is the main line curving round to East Stoke and Wool. *Anthony E. Trood*

Below:
Wareham-Worgret Junction-Swanage Gradient Profile.

Bottom:
With the 1 in 80 descent from Worgret Junction behind her, heading for Corfe Castle with the 12.04 to Swanage, Standard '4' tank No 80146 clatters across the iron viaduct over the River Frome, disturbing the peace of the rushes and reeds of the water meadows. For No 80146, hauling this midday working on Thursday 11 June 1964, there is a two-mile climb ahead of her at 1 in 78 to Furzebrook summit. *John Scrace*

run the Pike's tramway from the clay mines at Cotness, Povington and Creech via the Furzebrook works to Ridge Wharf on the River Frome. A straight half-mile stretch of line comes into view: out of the window — to the left — can be seen the slow mass of traffic on the main A351 road to Corfe and Swanage; in the distance a sparkling Poole Harbour basks in the glare of the sun. To the right, across the pine trees and gorse of the heath, rise the wooded slopes of Knowle Hill, a part of the Purbeck Hills.

The monotony of the straight is broken as the train clatters over one of the numerous farm crossings; pine trees cast cool shadows through the carriage windows. The train veers to the left over the spot where the Swanage branch would be cut short in the summer of 1972. It then sweeps under Norden's Catseye bridge — a graceful brick structure carrying the main A351 — then swerves right, past Norden Heath before rattling over the disused trackbed of the Middlebere tramway and gathering speed down the gradient through the Woodpecker cutting heading for Eldon's Siding, by this time sadly disused.

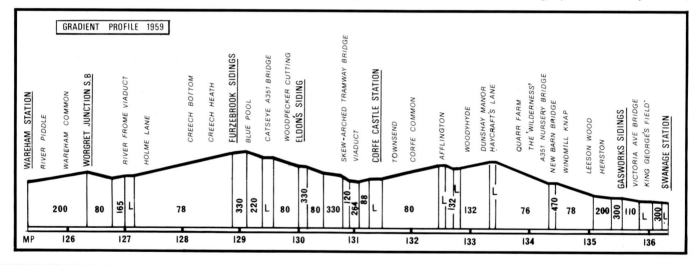

GRADIENT PROFILE 1959

The dappled landscape of woods and fields pass by whilst to the right of the train rises the choking heath. On the horizon, against the morning sun, the rugged outline of Corfe Castle can be glimpsed on several occasions. 'Rosie' and her 2-coach Maunsell 'push-pull' set gather speed past the gaunt shell of the trans-shipment shed for Eldon's Siding and a small sleeper-built track-ganger's hut. A 'Whistle' board and lattice post for Corfe's down distant signal — the yellow arm fixed at caution — flash past the window and No 30108, with a long shrill blast on her whistle, coasts under the

bridge carrying the lane to Slepe and Arne.

By the tramway sheds for Eldon's Siding, our train passes over the crossing which has latterly been used by lorries to collect ball clay from the Norden mines. With No 30108 still coasting we head into a tree-lined cutting before passing under the curious skew-arched bridge, which carries the old Fayle's tramway from the Norden mines to Eldon's Siding. With a sudden burst of sunlight the cutting is left behind and the magnificent vista of Corfe Castle — filling the gap between the hills — comes into view as our train sweeps down

the gradient, its brakes being steadily applied. With Jack leaning from the Maunsell's driving cab on this warm day we pass the Castle View Café — its car park already filled with cars and coaches, with trippers and hikers glancing upwards to watch our train pass by — and over the magnificent stone viaduct spanning the River Corfe — the confluence of two ancient streams, the Wicken and the Byle, as we run over the B3351 road to Rempstone and Studland. On this summer morning the cars on the A351 road below have come to a grinding halt whilst, above it all, the castle rises proud and noble. With the gorse-covered slopes of East Hill

Top left:
The Furzebrook ball clay sidings of Pike Brothers Fayle & Co on Saturday 27 August 1966, viewed from the road to East Creech, looking towards Norden and Corfe Castle. The points here were controlled from a ground frame unlocked by the Corfe Castle to Worgret Junction Key-Token. The old Pike's tramway to Ridge Wharf used to pass under the branch in the distance. Pike Brothers Fayle & Co were taken over by English China Clays in 1968. *C. L. Caddy*

Top right:
The end of the line by the Motala Kennels, Norden, on Friday 16 August 1986. It was here that the contractors lifting the branch for BR, Eagre & Co of Scunthorpe, ceased tracklifting operations during the third week of August 1972. This stopblock is now the furthest that BR penetrates Purbeck: beyond, towards Norden and Corfe Castle, is impenetrable undergrowth. *Andrew P. M. Wright*

Left:
After a 1/2-mile stretch of straight track from Furzebrook past the heath and pines around the beauty spot of Blue Pool, the branch suddenly swings left under the main A351 Wareham to Corfe road. Heading through a summer rain shower, No 34071 *601 Squadron* hauls the 09.15 Waterloo to Swanage towards the A351 Catseye bridge en route for Corfe Castle on Saturday 29 June 1963. No 34071's return working was the 13.23 Swanage to Waterloo which pulled into the Capital at 16.43. *D. Trevor Rowe*

Left:
Passing under the Catseye bridge, the branch curves right past Norden Heath heading for Eldon's Siding. On Sunday 7 May 1967, the LCGB ran the 'Dorset Coast Express' rail tour which included the Swanage branch. Here, on the second run with No 80011 at the rear, No 34023 *Blackmore Vale* rounds the curve and passes over Fayle's Middlebere tramway bound for Corfe Castle. This tramway connected the Norden clay pits with Poole Harbour. Built in 1806 it had become disused by World War 1. *John Scrace*

Below:
Corfe Castle Station Track Plan — 1956.

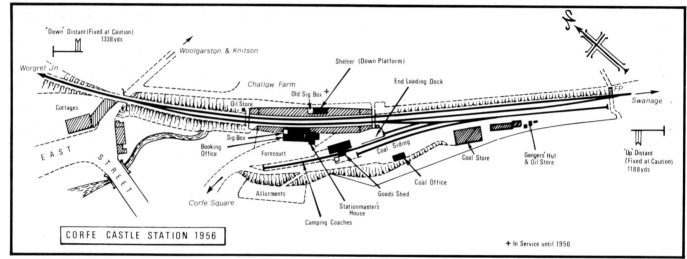

CORFE CASTLE STATION 1956

rising to the left and the cutting closing in, 'Rosie' propels our train through the cutting, its ragged walls only inches away from the carriage window, and over the girder bridge crossing the lane to Woolgarston. Past the stone rooftops of the village we gently pull up to the diminutive down platform. 'West Country' Bulleid Pacific No 34044 *Woolacombe*, pulling the 11.34 Swanage to Waterloo through train, hisses impatiently by the small signalbox on the up platform in front of a long rake of Bulleid coaches which stretch down to the far end of the passing loop. Corfe Signalman Bob Inman, in shirt sleeves, exchanges the Key-Token for the Tablet with Jack Spicer, crosses the tracks, inserts the Key-Token in the Tyer's No 7 machine, and after establishing that the line is clear, hands the Key-Token for the stretch of line to Worgret Junction to No 34044's Driver, Stan Symes.

With the castle dominating the scene, the up starting signal's red arm points to the sky and No 34044 eases her way out of the station bound for Waterloo. The tail lamp disappears as the train clatters over the girder bridge and is swallowed by the cutting. Our train — with Guard Alec Dudley aboard — blows its whistle and

Right:

Corfe Castle Signalling Diagram — January 1955.

Below left:

A typical scene on the Swanage branch. On Thursday 1 June 1950, a grimy unidentified 'M7', still in its SR livery, climbs the 1 in 80 gradient with the 13.33 from Swanage past Eldon's exchange siding; Eldon's Siding at Norden was 4 miles 6 chains from Worgret Junction. In tow is the usual LSWR 'push-pull' set with two new Bulleid main line coaches trailing; these were attached to an up London train at Wareham. Behind the train is the exchange shed, the down distant signal for Corfe Castle station and the overbridge for the road to Slepe and Arne. *J. C. Flemons*

Right:

After passing Eldon's Siding and the down distant signal for Corfe Castle, Standard tank No 80011 steams past the latter-day transfer point for the Norden clay mines whilst working a train to Corfe Castle and Swanage on Saturday 26 March 1966. The crossing visible behind the train was the scene of the branch's only accident which occurred in March 1962, when the 07.15 Swanage to Bournemouth ripped the back off a lorry that was not clear of the crossing. *D. Trevor Rowe*

Below:

A sight once familiar on the Swanage branch before it was strangled. During the fine early evening of Thursday 29 August 1963, the peace of the Corfe Gap is shattered by a double-headed through train from Swanage to the Midlands. With East Hill towering above and the view of Corfe Castle filling the carriage windows, 'M7' No 30048 pilots No 80081 out of Corfe Castle, with whistles blowing, bound for Wareham. The two branch coaches are coupled on the end of this 10-coach train; No 30048 and the Maunsell branch set were detached at Wareham. Just a decade later there would be no railway here at all — just a swathe of weed-infested ballast. *Rodney A. Lissenden*

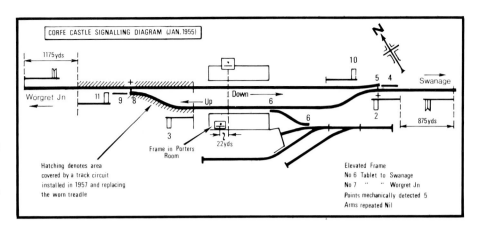

Jack steadily eases 'Rosie' away from the platform. Porter/Signalman Ernie Petter watches from the opposite platform, as the station master's house and then the station's enamel sign disappear from sight past our carriage window. We pick up speed past the goods shed and end-loading dock with a line of coal wagons in the yard, passing L. G. Stockley's (the coal merchant) and the loading gauge before clattering over the points, passing the up home signal and tackling the 1 in 80 climb out of Corfe Castle. As we round the curve towards Townsend, Corfe Common comes into view with Kingston village church, designed by the renowned Victorian architect G. E. Street, on the skyline. Soon it is the up distant signal for Corfe Castle, the sweep round the curve towards the Afflington road bridge, and then the climb

Left:
Viewed from the castle walls, 'M7' No 30060's bark interrupts the summer tranquility of Corfe Castle as she accelerates across the handsome Purbeck stone viaduct over the B3351 Studland road with the 11.34am to Wareham on a fine Saturday in July 1958. In tow is the LSWR push-pull set and two through coaches for the London train trailing. In the distance is Wytch Farm and Poole Harbour. *Peter Q. Treloar*

Below left:
On Thursday 29 August 1963, 'M7' No 30048 steams across the Corfe viaduct propelling Maunsell 'push-pull' set No 603 on a morning train from Wareham to Swanage. With the main A351 Wareham to Swanage road to the left, the train is about to pass through the East Hill cutting before pulling into Corfe station. On the skyline is the skew-arched bridge which carried the tramway between the Norden mines and Eldon's Siding. *Rodney A. Lissenden*

up through a cutting before plunging under the A351 Swanage road and descending past Woodyhyde.

The Langton Matravers quarries are just visible on the skyline, as we coast round past Dunshay Manor and over the branch's second summit — Haycraft's Lane over-bridge — at Harman's Cross. From here it is all downhill. With the bungalows of Harman's Cross visible through the windows to the left, and the cottages of Langton Matravers silhouetted against the

summer sky to the right, No 30108 coasts down the 1 in 78 incline, passes over another farm crossing at Quarr Farm before steaming through the woods of the Wilderness. We come to the end of this long straight and veer left over yet another farm crossing, passing under the Valley Road Nursery bridge before we squeeze through a sandy cutting and emerge again into the glorious sunshine. We rattle over the tiny girder bridge at New Barn Farm at a slow 25mph; 'Rosie' once again picks up speed as she approaches Leeson Wood en route for Herston, making two graceful sweeps, first right and then left.

In the distance, the houses of Herston Cross and Swanage can be discerned above the oak trees; as the bogies jar over the fishplates, we continue sweeping left before passing under a handsome stone overbridge that carries the Washpond Lane to Godlingston and its ancient brickworks, which would still be producing bricks in 1986. After Herston, the gas-works can be seen in the distance and soon we are coasting round the curve past the Swanage distant signal — unusual with its wooden arm — and the site of the old gasworks' sidings, which had been lifted just seven years before. We pass under the Victoria Avenue road bridge and through the outskirts of Swanage. Our genial Guard, Alec Dudley, exchanges a wave with his wife in the back garden of their house in King's Road West which over-looks the line as our train steams by. With King George's playing fields to the left and

the back gardens of the houses along King's Road West to the right, George Burt's Purbeck House is visible on the skyline. 'Rosie' slackens speed, curves left across the stream bridge and past the old engine shed, turntable, coaling dock and water tower — all dwarfed by the tall elm trees by the cemetery. Under the North-brook bridge the large station yard can be seen, with Standard '4' 2-6-0 No 76019 steaming contentedly by the old weigh-bridge; she is engaged in shunting and station pilot duties before working back up the branch. Leaning from the driving compartment of the Maunsell coach, Jack Spicer — with his familiar cap on — hands the pouch (containing the Tablet for the Corfe Castle to Swanage block section) to Signalman Arthur Galton, who is standing to receive it beside the beautifully pro-portioned LSWR signalbox. As we con-tinue decelerating, the starting signal for the main platform is passed, with the bay track and long goods shed behind. Finally, the 1930s enamel 'Swanage' sign and the waiting passengers on the platform come into view, while our fellow passengers — the children clasping their buckets and spades — expectantly look out of the carriage windows at a sun-drenched Swanage as our trip comes to an end.

At last, our 11.30 from Wareham eases past the station master's house and pulls up under the 1938 platform canopy at 11.56 — dead on time. We disembark into the diffused sunlight of the platform; it is a hive of activity with staff scurrying round

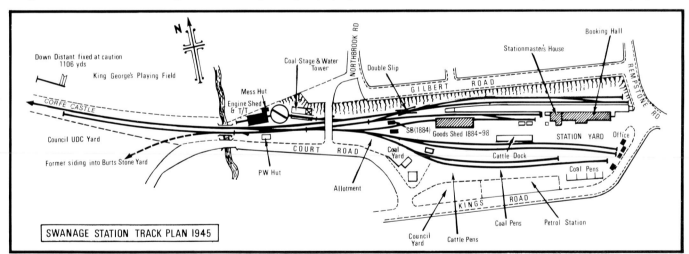

Above:
Swanage Station Track Plan — 1945.

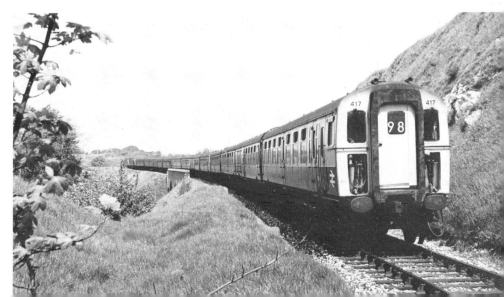

Right:
A scene reminiscent of the long troop trains of the war years. After regular through services ceased on Friday 3 October 1969, the extremely popular excursion and ramblers' specials still ran to Corfe and Swanage. Here, on Sunday 24 May 1970, a 12-coach train (composed of three 4-TC sets and double-headed by two Class 33s on the Wareham end) snakes its way over the viaduct and passes through the narrow cutting before arriving at Corfe Castle station. 4-TC set No 417 carries the usual branch headcode '98'. *Anthony E. Trood*

attentively. The sound of chatter strikes our ears. Amidst the bustle, 'Rosie' basks in the noonday sun, simmering patiently and ready for her next departure for Corfe Castle and Wareham. The sun plays on the leaves of the trees by the buffer stops. Beside 'Rosie', and with the smell of coal dust, lubricating oil and steam, Jack Spicer chats with Alec Dudley whilst Keith Sloper watches the fire and checks the level of the coal in No 30108's bunker. The Station Master, Mr Walden, loiters on the platform keeping an eye on the goings-on. By the parcels office, newly-arrived Station Foreman, Jack Cannons, has a word with Porter Bill 'Taffy' Hazell. The crush of passengers file along beneath the station clock, the hanging baskets of flowers and the enamel station signs. A lady buys a newspaper from Mrs Cook at H. G. Cook's bookstall whilst another browses through the paperbacks. We pass into the cool, tiled booking hall, handing our tickets to Porter/Shunter George Sims. As we process through the main doors on to the station forecourt — with Bull's taxis waiting expectantly for business — a long line of Bulleid coaches stand in the yard by the beach hut offices of the coal merchants. These will form the 13.15 up Waterloo train this afternoon. To the right is the station master's house and the five-bar gate leading to the yard, the foreman's office and the goods shed. Turning left, with taxis departing amidst the bustle, we join our fellow passengers to walk past the Bell & Cronin indicator board and souvenir stall crammed with seaside trivia, before reaching Station Road opposite the Railway Hotel. The smell of salt is in the air and the beach is a mere three minutes' walk away.

Right:
Through trains to Corfe Castle and Swanage were always of interest, connecting quiet rural Purbeck with the hustle and bustle of the Capital. On Saturday 11 June 1966, the 09.15 Waterloo to Swanage was running late; finally, two hours late, rebuilt Pacific No 34025 *Whimple* draws into Corfe Castle station past the up starter signal at 14.21. No 34025 was built in 1946, rebuilt in October 1957, and finally withdrawn in July 1967. *John R. Coleman*

Below:
Corfe Castle station viewed from the castle. On a glorious summer evening in 1963, 'M7' No 30108 'Rosie' leaves the village with her 2-coach Maunsell set bound for Wareham and is about to disappear into the cutting through East Hill. In the foreground is the tortuous A351 main Wareham to Swanage road as it skirts round the old mill where, until the 1950s, flour was ground by the Corfe bakers, the Battricks. *Bryan H. Kimber*

Above:
On Monday 8 June 1964, Ivatt 'Mickey Mouse' tank No 41270 coasts through the East Hill cutting, over the lane to Challow Farm, Woolgarston and Knitson and into Corfe station with the 3-coach 16.57 from Wareham. The cottage snuggling against the embankment is 'Cromwell Cottage', so named after the leader of the Parliamentary forces which captured and wrecked Corfe Castle during the English Civil War in 1646. No 41270 was built at Crewe in 1949 and fitted with 'push-pull' equipment; however, by 1964 this was not used, No 41270 running round her Maunsell coaches at Swanage and Wareham. *John Scrace*

Below:
Class M7, No 30108 'Rosie' makes a conscientious departure from Corfe Castle's down platform propelling her Maunsell 'push-pull' set with the 15.15 for Swanage on the sunny afternoon of Sunday 7 July 1963. To the right, under the station canopy, Porter/Signalman Ernie Petter watches the departure. In the distance is the small goods yard whilst, behind the train, is the village dairy next to Challow Farm. *C. L. Caddy*

Above:
On a sunny day in July 1962, Maunsell 'Q' 0-6-0 No 30541 draws the midday branch freight out of Corfe Castle past the main station buildings bound for Wareham. No 30541 worked freight duties on the Swanage branch for many years until transferred to Guildford in March 1963. Withdrawn in November 1964 and consigned to Barry Scrapyard, she was rescued in 1974 and is now preserved by the Maunsell Locomotive Society on the Bluebell Railway. *W. Philip Conolly*

Left:
Whilst working the 09.50 to Swanage on Wednesday 24 August 1966, the crew of No 80019 and Swanage Guard Alec Dudley, pose for the photographer during their brief stop at the down platform. No 80019 had spent the night in the engine shed at Swanage, her first duty being the 07.40 to Wareham. She then worked the branch for the whole day before running empty train to Poole from Wareham at 20.20, and light engine thence to Bournemouth MPD at 20.45.
Anthony E. Trood

Above:
On the afternoon of Monday 30 August 1971 — the last summer of a working Swanage branch — Corfe Signalman, the late Arthur Galton, chats with a senior resident of the village, Miss Record. In the distance a 10-coach train clatters over the points and snakes into the loop from Swanage. This was the return working of an Oxford-Swanage excursion. Behind Miss Record is the station signalbox, built as an extension to the porters' lobby in 1956, which replaced the original signalbox on the down platform.
Anthony E. Trood

Right:
On the warm afternoon of Sunday 7 July 1963, Relief Signalman Frank Kitcatt cleans his Volkswagen Beetle on the station forecourt. To the left are the signalbox and toilets, then the booking hall with the waiting room and ladies toilet and station master's house with, to the far right, the gate leading to the end-loading dock and goods shed. *C. L. Caddy*

Below right:
A deserted Corfe Castle station looking towards Wareham on a fine summer's evening in 1948, with the original 1884 signalbox attached to the waiting shelter on the down platform. As always, the East Hill of the Purbeck Hills dominates the scene. The whole of the Swanage branch track was relaid in the winter of 1947 to make up for the arrears in maintenance built up since the late 1930s.
Lens of Sutton

Above:
Three-coach 'Hampshire' DEMU No 1128 idles at the down platform whilst working the 15.35 Wareham to Swanage train on Thursday 7 August 1969. By this time the station displayed a heavy air of neglect and decay. The station had been de-staffed (except for the two Signalmen, Bob Richards and Arthur Galton) on Sunday 8 September 1968. No 1128 was originally built in 1960 for service on the Salisbury to Reading line and is still attached to Eastleigh depot. *John Scrace*

Below:
Corfe Castle station between trains on Saturday 6 June 1964, viewed from the Swanage end of the down platform. To the left is the goods shed and the point into the goods yard, closed on Monday 4 October 1965. Behind the 1930s enamel station sign is one of the extremely popular camping coaches, 12-wheeler No P52, ex-Car 98 which was built in 1921 for the SECR services as the first-class car *Milan*. Both coaches were broken up where they stood in the spring of 1968.
John Scrace

Left:

On Christmas Eve, 1971, with just eight days of operation remaining, Corfe Signalman Bob Richards receives the Swanage to Corfe Staff and hands the Corfe to Worgret Junction Key-Token to the driver of No 1128 working a train to Wareham. Visible in the cab is a young Corfe Castle resident, Peter Frost. He regularly rode in the cabs of the DEMUs; little did he realise that he would be driving steam engines on the Swanage Railway in the 1980s. Bob Richards started his railway career at Corfe Castle on Monday 16 April 1962. *Anthony E. Trood*

Below:

Class M7 No 30052, with Driver Jack Spicer at the controls, drifts along the Corfe loop with a Maunsell 'push-pull' set in tow on a train from Swanage on Thursday 29 August 1963. Viewed from the end-loading dock, the cramped goods yard is well shown with the sidings to the end-loading dock, goods shed and coal siding leading off the long headshunt. No 30052 first ran in Purbeck in April 1963, was withdrawn in May 1964 and cut up the following October at Briton Ferry, Glamorgan. *Rodney A. Lissenden*

Above:

Corfe station viewed from the position of the train in the previous photograph, but just six years later on Sunday 6 April 1969. The goods yard lies partially lifted deep amongst the weeds. With the castle towering over the station, a special Waterloo to Swanage train, made up of 4-TC sets Nos 407 and 426 with Class 33 No D6580 on the Wareham end, stands at the down platform. *Anthony E. Trood*

Below:

A dramatic departure at Corfe. With the gaunt castle towering above, attracting a good deal of attention, unrebuilt 'West Country' Pacific No 34023 *Blackmore Vale* blasts away from the down platform for the second time that day, past the raised starter signal bound for Swanage with the 'Dorset Coast Express' at 14.53 on Sunday 7 May 1967. The passing loop at Corfe Castle was lengthened by 4 chains towards Swanage during December 1943. *John H. Bird*

On Friday 12 June 1964, Standard tank No 80146 steams away from Corfe Castle station and up the 1 in 80 incline with the 12.04 to Swanage heading for Townsend and Afflington. This was a marvellous spot in the steam days from which to watch 'West Country' Pacifics depart for Swanage with their long London trains. It was hardly the same with the advent of the moaning and juddering DEMU.
John Scrace

With Corfe Castle approaching, and still at a gradient of 1 in 80, 3-coach 'Hampshire' DEMU No 1114 coasts down the incline past Townsend with the 11.16 to Wareham on Monday 31 August 1971. From Tuesday 6 June 1967, the line between Corfe and Swanage was worked as an unsignalled 'long siding' under One Train regulations with a Staff. No 1114 consumed 6gal of diesel fuel on each single trip on the branch and had, like all 'Hampshire' units, buck-eye couplings and automatic air and electro-pneumatic brakes.
Anthony E. Trood

Left:
Exactly one year later things had changed radically. Here, on the curve across Corfe Common towards Afflington bridge the contractors Eagre & Co, have been at work lifting the branch after its closure. Rails and chairs have been thrown in the cess. The sleepers await the JCBs to drag them out of the ballast and load them on to articulated lorries. The up distant for Corfe Castle has lost its arm. Ahead is the main A351 road to Swanage at Afflington.
Robert J. Richards

Below:
A scene familiar on the Swanage branch for more than 30 years which will always last in the memory. 'M7' No 30480 and Maunsell 'push-pull' set climb the 1 in 132 gradient up from Woodyhyde before steaming under the Afflington road bridge and coasting down the 1 in 80 into Corfe Castle with an afternoon train on the rather wet Saturday of 29 June 1963. Behind the train the line dips past Woodyhyde before climbing to Harman's Cross. On the skyline are the stone quarries of Langton Matravers.
D. Trevor Rowe

Left:
The branch's second summit at Haycraft's Lane, Harman's Cross, was two miles from Corfe Castle and three from Swanage. It is now the site of the Swanage Railway Project's second halt. On Saturday 30 July 1966, Ivatt 'Teddy Bear' tank No 41230, having climbed at 1 in 132, descends at 1 in 76 towards Quarr Farm and New Barn with the 10.47 to Swanage on the day that England won the World Cup at Wembley. *Lawrence S. Golden*

Centre left:
With the bungalows of Harman's Cross and the Purbeck Hills in the background, a rebuilt 'Battle of Britain' Pacific storms up the 1 in 76 gradient between Quarr Farm and Haycraft's Lane with the 11.34 Swanage to Waterloo on Saturday 30 July 1966. Just over 20 years later the Swanage Railway Project's track relaying train passed here heading for Haycraft's Lane. *Lawrence S. Golden*

Below:
One summer day in 1963, 'M7' No 30107 determinedly tackles the 1 in 76 gradient between the A351 Nursery bridge and the current Pondarosa Farm crossing with an early morning train from Swanage for Corfe Castle. No 30107 was built in 1905 and had the distinction of being the very last 'M7' to work a train on the Swanage branch on the morning of Saturday 9 May 1964. *Mike Esau*

Left:

The trackbed at New Barn was always unstable, being regularly visited by ballast trains up until 1972. With branch steam ousted, many steam rail tours featured the branch in 1967. On Saturday 25 March 1967, Ivatt tank No 41320 hauls the MRTS's 'Hants and Dorset Branch Flyer' between the New Barn and Nursery bridges heading for Corfe Castle and Wareham. *Martyn Thresh*

Below:

Just under a mile from New Barn, Driver Jock Hapgood looks nonchalantly from the footplate of 'M7' No 30107 whilst working a Swanage-Corfe train past Washpond Lane bridge, Herston, during the summer of 1963. The concrete track through here, between Victoria Avenue and New Barn, was laid in the summer of 1956. The Swanage Railway Project's halt at Herston, opened in 1984, is just beyond the bridge seen here. *Mike Esau*

Right:

On Saturday 24 March 1962, 'M7' 0-4-4T No 30328 steams under the Victoria Avenue bridge as she accelerates through the outskirts of Swanage with an afternoon train for Corfe and Wareham. Until 1956, the old gasworks siding used to leave the branch on the Corfe side of this bridge. *C. L. Caddy*

Below right:

From Victoria Avenue bridge the line runs into Swanage station at 1 in 110 and 1 in 300. On Saturday 30 July 1966, Standard '4' No 80134 gathers speed out of Swanage with the 14.28 for Wareham. In tow are two BR Mk 1 coaches. No 80134 was built at Brighton in 1955, first worked to Swanage in October 1964 and was withdrawn from Bournemouth MPD in July 1967. *C. L. Caddy*

Right:

**Standard '4' 2-6-0 No 76013 accelerates
round the concrete-sleepered curve out of
Swanage station past King George's Field,
heading for Victoria Avenue, Herston and
beyond, with the branch freight for Corfe
Castle on the morning of Tuesday 9 June
1964. The branch goods service ceased 16
months later on Monday 4 October 1965.**
John Scrace

Below:

**Type 3 diesel No D6507 runs past Swanage
station's engine shed and turntable with
the 10.45 from Waterloo early on the
afternoon of Saturday 27 August 1966.
No 80019 simmers in the headshunt as
No D6507 passes. No 80019 later pulled
the stock off No D6507, placing the
carriages in the yard before returning light
engine with No D6507 to Wareham that
afternoon.** *C. L. Caddy*

Far right:

**Built in 1905 and withdrawn in May 1964,
'M7' No 30107 does not look her age as she
basks in the Swanage sun of July 1962,
beside the coal dock and water tower one
lunchtime. The water tower (built by
Brown & Bobby Engineers of London) and
the 50ft turntable were cut up for scrap in
November 1967, when most of the
station's tracks were lifted. This scene will
be repeated when No 30053 returns to
Swanage from Steamtown, USA.**
W. Philip Conolly

Above:
In charge of the 09.50 from Wareham, No 80146 coasts under the Northbrook Road bridge with her fireman preparing to hand the Corfe to Swanage Tablet, in its pouch, to the signalman at Swanage on Thursday 11 June 1964. The point to the left led to the goods yard and goods shed. No 80146 had worked the branch since December 1963, was withdrawn in July 1967 and scrapped in early 1968.
John Scrace

Below:
Swanage Signalman Jimmy Hunt waits to catch the Tablet from the Bournemouth fireman of 'Battle of Britain' Pacific No 34060 *25 Squadron* as she steams into the station with the 09.15 from Waterloo one Saturday in August 1965. Jimmy Hunt, having started at Swanage in the 1950s and witnessed the rundown of the branch, left BR in March 1967. He still lives in Swanage and watches, with a touch of irony, the rebuilding of the branch on which he had worked for so long.
Courtesy of James Hunt

Right:
Swanage signalbox, built in late 1884, viewed from Gilbert Road on the evening of Saturday 17 June 1967, the day before the branch's last steam train of all ran down from Wareham. Closed on Tuesday 6 June 1967, the box was demolished in November 1967, with its 23-lever frame being sold for scrap to Channel Metals Ltd of Poole. Swanage's last Signalman, the late Arthur Galton, was transferred to Corfe Castle when the box closed. Behind the box are the two remaining tracks leading to the goods yard. *George M. Moon*

Below:
The Lady and the Maid. On the fine afternoon of Saturday 15 August 1959, Drummond '700' 0-6-0 No 30695 (of a class introduced in 1897) pauses at the entrance to Swanage's goods yard during shunting and pilot duties, as rebuilt 'West Country' No 34042 *Dorchester* (built in 1946) prepares to depart the main platform with the 13.23 to Waterloo. Since these long trains fouled the track circuits and treadles, they had to be signalled off with flags. In the foreground is the station master's allotment. *George M. Moon*

Left:
Swanage station viewed from Gilbert Road one summer evening. No 80019, after working the 17.02 from Bournemouth Central and running round via the loop, prepares to leave with the 18.17 to Wareham on Monday 30 May 1966. Behind the train is the bay platform and goods shed. Signalman Arthur Galton chats to No 80019's crew. *C. L. Caddy*

Centre left:
On a Sunday early in July 1966, Standard '4' No 76014 and her Swanage crew depart the bay platform past the disused goods shed and yard with the 17.57 for Corfe Castle and Wareham. In the main platform, Brush Type 4 locomotive No D1686 waits to haul the 8-coach 18.12 Swanage-Eastleigh. Beside No 76014 is the complicated double-slip pointwork, originally installed in 1897. *Chris Phillips*

Below:
Crew changes at Swanage on the last Saturday of branch steam. Rebuilt 'West Country' Pacific No 34004 *Yeovil* simmers at the end of the main platform with the 11.20 to Waterloo on Saturday 3 September 1966. On the bay track, Ivatt tank No 41316 steams past the signalbox and goods shed with the 10.47 from Wareham. No 34004 arrived at Swanage after double-heading the 10.05 from Wareham with No 80134. No 34004 then drew the stock from the yard, propelling it into the main platform. *Anthony E. Trood*

Above:
On a beautiful sunny Sunday, the fireman attends to the tender whilst Driver Jock Hapgood enjoys the sunshine; Standard '4' 2-6-0 No 76014 waits at Swanage's main platform to haul the 12.30 to Wareham on Sunday 3 July 1966. Jock, due to the impending dieselisation, retired three months early, in September 1966. It was the end, too, for No 76014 which was withdrawn the same month from Bournemouth MPD. *A. B. Tompkins*

Right:
Ivatt tank No 41316 simmers in the bay platform at Swanage after arriving with the 10.47 from Wareham on Saturday 3 September 1966. In the yard, beyond the lifted goods shed siding, Standard tank No 80138 simmers by the old weighbridge. In the main platform, the 11.20 to Waterloo prepares to depart whilst No 41316's Bournemouth crew chat with Guard Alec Dudley and No 34004's erstwhile Driver and Fireman on the last Saturday of Swanage branch steam.
Anthony E. Trood

Above:

**The end of the Swanage branch. After
arriving with the 12.16 from Wareham and
Corfe Castle on Saturday 27 August 1966,
Ivatt tank No 41312 draws forward before
running round her stock via the loop to the
right. The 1938 station canopy, lamp and
gas rooms are to the left. The run-round
loop was lifted in November 1967 after
being abolished that June. No 41312 is
now preserved at Caerphilly, South
Wales.** *Martyn Thresh*

Left:

**The station master's house, designed by
Galbraith & Church, with the 1938
extended booking hall beyond, on Monday
13 July 1970, viewed from the station
yard. The gate on to the platform is to the
left. Boarded up in 1972, and nearly
demolished to make way for a shopping
centre, the buildings reverted to their old
function in February 1976, when taken
over by the Swanage Railway Project.**
John Scrace

THE SWANAGE BRANCH

2   Efforts to build a Swanage branch line 1847-85

The first scheme for a standard gauge railway to penetrate the introverted Isle of Purbeck appeared in 1847 as a branch line off the Southampton and Dorchester main line at the market town of Wareham. Although it was envisaged that it would serve the stone industry around Swanage, Langton and Worth Matravers, the plan was never proceeded with. The year 1861 saw the LSWR sponsor another proposal for a Purbeck railway — this time to serve the clay mines around Creech. This, too, failed since the line's trajectory would have split Wareham's ancient walls in two. Another factor in its failure, as with the 1847 proposal, was Purbeck's landed

gentry who were (and it seems still are, over 120 years later) distinctly anti-railway, as they feared the coming of the liberating railway would loosen their grip over Purbeck's rural population; the gentry also had a large vested interest in the stone and ball clay industries on the Isle. The clay mines around Creech, Furzebrook and Norden had solved their transportation problems by building their own narrow gauge lines from the pits across the heaths to the shores of Poole Harbour, where the clay was shipped away. All this was neat and tidy, and well within the control of the mine owners, Pike Bros of Furzebrook and Fayle & Co of Norden.

In 1862 there was a further proposal for a line, this time tendered by the Isle of Purbeck Railway Co, with the aim of serving the growing seaside town of Swanage along the lines of the defunct 1847 plan. Supported by the LSWR,

Below:
Station Master George Parsons poses with his staff for Swanage photographer William Powell on the platform in about 1900. Behind them is the station master's house and original 1884 canopy. The Railway Hotel is visible in the distance. Mr Parsons was the first station master in May 1885; the last was Harry Newman in 1966.
Courtesy of Bournemouth Evening Echo

opposition came from the worthy burghers of Wareham, until they were appeased by the proposed provision of a separate station south of the town and goods exchange facilities with the wharves on the River Frome. With these 'Wareham Clauses' the Bill was lodged in Parliament, was passed and received the Royal Assent from Queen Victoria on 22 June 1863.

However, there were still problems regarding the breaking of Wareham's Roman and Anglo-Saxon walls. With opposition from landowners and financial support not forthcoming, the Act had lapsed by 1868. At this time it should be remembered that the only way of travelling from the main line station at Wareham to Corfe Castle and Swanage was by an uncomfortable 12-mile coach journey via Corfe Castle and Kingston — there being no valley road through Harman's Cross at this time. However, despite Purbeck not having a railway, Swanage continued to grow with a vengeance, catered for by steamboat services from Bournemouth, Poole and Weymouth.

In 1877 another proposal was put forward that would tap not only the rich stone and ball clay traffic, but also the growing potential of the seaside holiday market. The leading promoter was George Burt, a notable and proud resident of Swanage, who was keen to see his town profit from a railway link with the outside world. He and John Mowlem, founder of the world-renowned construction company (who died in 1868), had been behind the 1863 proposal. The 1877 plan put forward two alternative routes: the first dated back to 1863, with the railway diverging from the station at Northport, and passing Wareham's walls at Westport, where there would be another station; crossing the Frome, the branch would run parallel to the causeway, ending up at Stoborough, where another station would be built, before running parallel to the current A351 road to Furzebrook, Norden and Corfe Castle.

The second route completely 'went round' the problem; namely the branch would diverge from the main line some 1¼ miles west of Wareham at the hamlet of Worgret. It would then pass over the River Frome before continuing through East Holme and Creech Bottom, resuming the route taken by the first proposal at Furzebrook. Thus, Wareham's walls would be safe — George Burt thought he had cracked it! However, the Wareham residents were still opposed to a railway for Corfe and Swanage. George Burt held negotiations with the LSWR but there were problems about the working of the line once completed. George Burt, of Purbeck House, Swanage, did not give up: he probed public opinion. Alas, comments were not favourable; the people of Swanage seemed ignorant of the considerable advantages a line would bring to their town. Nevertheless, he renewed negotiations with the LSWR with the result that in November 1880 a Bill was lodged in Parliament.

The next step was to convince Purbeck people that a railway would be beneficial, something that proved to be an uphill task. The route via Worgret, Holme and Creech seemed the only one that might succeed. George Burt enlisted expert help in the form of Mr Galbraith of Messrs Galbraith & Church, Consulting Engineers to the LSWR, to survey the route and estimate the costs of construction. A meeting was held on 4 December 1880 at the Mowlem Institute, Swanage, to enlist support. Even though only 30 Swanage worthies attended, Mr Galbraith swung the meeting with his authority and, in an incredible change of heart, the meeting concluded that the proposed Swanage Railway would be 'highly beneficial to the town'. With this unanimous agreement a committee of notable Swanage residents was set up to liaise with the promoters in obtaining an Act, and in raising the required capital for the project. With local politics settled, capital of £90,000 in £10 shares was raised and a further £30,000 through loans, if required.

It is ironic that problems seem to be the norm in Swanage, both over building the line in the 1870s and 1880s, and in the rebuilding of the Swanage Railway in the 1970s and 1980s! The Bill (lodged in Parliament in November 1880) passed through the Commons and the Lords

Above left:
The LSWR driver and fireman pose on '46' class Adams tank locomotive No 133 at Wareham's main down platform 2, before working a train to Corfe Castle and Swanage c1900. No 133 of Eastleigh shed had been built by Beyer Peacock in July 1879, rebuilt as a 4-4-2T in January 1885 and placed on the duplicate list in March 1903. She was scrapped in 1921. Sub-shedded at Bournemouth, these locomotives were nicknamed 'Hamworthy Buses'. *Courtesy of Wareham Museum*

Left:
In the years preceding World War 1, a Class 0415 Adams 4-4-2T coasts through the East Hill cutting and into Corfe station under the shadow of the castle with a train from Wareham to Swanage. Compare this with the picture on page 49 of the very last BR train running into Corfe Castle on Friday 23 June 1972.
Courtesy of Henry Casserley Collection

during the first half of July 1881, with Queen Victoria finally giving her Royal Assent on Thursday 8 July 1881, to 'The Swanage Railway Act, 1881'. This gave authority for two lines to be built: the main branch line from Wareham to Swanage via Worgret and Corfe Castle, and a narrow gauge tramway from the terminus along the south side of what is now Station Road to the Swanage Pier Tramway — a line which carried stone and coal from the pier to near the Mowlem Institute. It was originally intended that a narrow gauge line would join the extension from the quarries at Langton Matravers.

With the Swanage Railway Co formed, its chairman was naturally George Burt, whilst other directors on the board were W. Lansdowne-Beale and John Charles Robinson. The other two directors were Stephen Soames and C. E. Mortimer, with their positions being confirmed by the shareholders. An appendix to the Act agreed that the branch would be worked by the LSWR from its opening; a further interesting aspect was that since the Swanage branch would be a feeder for the LSWR's main line, thus bringing them more revenue, 4% of the cost of building the branch would be annually paid to the Swanage Railway Co. The Swanage Railway Co would purchase the required land, build the line and maintain it — with the exception of the permanent way, which was to be the responsibility of the LSWR. After the first year of operation, the LSWR was obliged to work the branch as if it were their own, with the option of buying it from the Swanage Railway Co.

With legalities settled, attention was turned to building the line itself. The Swanage Railway Co, with George Burt at its helm, contracted Messrs Galbraith and Church to survey the route and draw up the necessary specifications and plans. They estimated the costs of construction would amount to around £77,000, not including rails, which had already been acquired by the railway company. Tenders were then invited, five being received ranging from £76,646 to £92,995, with the lowest tender being submitted by Curry & Reeves of Westminster. Being close to Galbraith & Church's estimate, their tender was accepted. Construction of the Swanage branch started on Friday 5 June 1883, with the first sod being cut on the site of Swanage station. Curry & Reeves were contracted to build the line, with E. G. Perkins of Lymington sub-contracted to build the two iron viaducts over the River Frome, near Worgret Junction, and to build the railway between Worgret Junction and Corfe Castle. Severe trouble was encountered in digging the Furzebrook cutting through Creech Heath: the sand and clay formation was so heavy that the cutting had to be hand-dug using spudgels.

The cutting through the East Hill of the Purbecks at Corfe Castle also proved difficult during construction, the chalk strata having to be blasted with dynamite. It is said that these operations resulted in portions falling off the Norman Castle. The buildings on the branch were constructed by Bull & Co of Southampton from Purbeck stone. The initial plans made provision for a third track to be laid between Wareham station and Worgret Junction, adjacent to the LSWR main line, so that branch trains could have an independent track into Wareham station.

Above:

Swanage station and yard from the Northbrook bridge one summer's evening shortly after World War 1. The main platform, station buildings and goods shed are to the left, with the extensive yard to the right. The crossover between the bay platform track and the goods shed siding was lifted in December 1945. The signalman was forbidden to berth bogie coaches in the far siding No 6 for lack of clearance. *Lens of Sutton*

This would obviate the need for points, which would have cost the company some £500.

To this end, a Parliamentary Notice appeared in the *Sherborne Journal* stating that the LSWR intended to apply for the acquisition of land lying next to the existing main line, 'for the extra line of rails in connection with the Swanage Railway, and for a new railway station at Northport'. The Friday 16 January 1885 edition of the *Wareham and Isle of Purbeck Advertiser* said that 'although the company will purchase land for making the third line of rails from the Worgret Junction of the Swanage line (to Wareham), it is not expected this will be carried out for some considerable time'. In fact, this was never done, although the new Wareham station — complete with bay platforms for Swanage trains — was built during 1886 and early 1887. The Swanage Railway Co's financial position was good compared with other contemporary schemes. On Sunday 18 February 1885, the day after the completion of Swanage station, a half-yearly general meeting was held at which George Burt was chairman. The directors felt sure that the line would be complete for handing over to the LSWR by May of that year. Accounts showed that all of the £90,000 worth of shares had been produced. Of the £30,000 that could be raised as loans, £12,000 worth of debentures had been issued with some £18,000 still available.

By the autumn of 1884, the Purbeck area was eagerly awaiting the coming of the railway. The *Wareham and Isle of Purbeck Advertiser* for 17 October 1884 noted the progress towards completion of the Swanage branch line. 'A large quantity of materials, chairs, rails etc are being daily conveyed from the station yard towards Corfe Castle by the locomotive engine, and, as one rides along some five miles, one can scarcely yet realise he is actually in Purbeck running along at such a speed on a line towards one of the most naturally beautiful seaside retreats on the South coast. . . Thanks to the directors of the new railway. . . Swanage will be united with England.'

All the overbridges along the branch were built to accommodate double track if required, with enough land also being purchased for that purpose. The bridges between Worgret Junction and the Catseye bridge at Norden, were built of brick, with all those bridges between Norden and Swanage being constructed of Purbeck stone. The magnificent viaduct of Purbeck stone at Corfe Castle was only built to accommodate a single track. Such was the effect of the new Swanage branch that the Ship Hotel and the Temperance Hotel in Corfe Castle were enlarged in 1885/86 to cater for the new railway traffic. The renowned Victorian architect, G. E. Street, who designed Kingston's grand church some two miles south of Corfe Castle, was of the opinion that when the railway came to Purbeck the stone carried on the branch would be used in six out of every seven churches built in Great Britain.

In the first few days of May 1885 the final touches were being made to the completed branch line, with the last quick-set hedges being planted just within the lineside fences to help soften the effect of this short-term scar on Purbeck's landscape. George Burt and Swanage were determined that the first public train on the branch would run from Swanage station. To this end, a Beattie 2-4-0WT was off-loaded at the 1847 Wareham station and on to a trailer for the 10-mile horse-drawn journey to Swanage. The branch's first engine was hauled via Stoborough, Norden, Corfe Castle, Kingston, Langton Matravers (there being no valley road through Harman's Cross at this time) and Herston before arriving at

Swanage station. A team of 24 carthorses was required to haul Purbeck's first 'iron horse' up the hill to Kingston. The entourage left Wareham on a Thursday morning and reached Swanage one day later. The Beattie Well Tank was steamed at the small coal dock the following Tuesday for her trial run before working the first train between Swanage, Corfe Castle and Wareham.

Tuesday 5 May was the day of the formal inspection of the new Swanage branch line by the Board of Trade. All aspects and structures were strictly inspected and local rumours abounded that all was not well. However, Major Marindin of the Board of Trade was satisfied with what he saw. Accompanying him were E. W. Verrinder, Traffic Superintendent, J. Dredge, Engineer, and J. C. Holliday, District Superintendent — all of whom were from the LSWR. Also inspecting the line on this occasion were E. Tinsley, Station Master at Wareham, and Messrs Church, Francis and Jones representing the engineer's contractors. Local dignitaries and other guests were also invited, all boarding a special saloon for the journey down the branch line. The entourage left Wareham's 1847 station at 9.30am, with the train stopping at Worgret Junction, the viaducts over the River Frome, as well as Corfe Castle and Swanage stations. Furthermore, the train stopped at all structures, bridges and signals. After lunch in Swanage, the train departed from the terminus at 2.50pm for the return journey, this time stopping briefly at Corfe Castle before arriving back at Wareham at 3.20pm.

On Saturday 16 May 1885 George Burt the company chairman, with his fellow directors and invited guests, travelled down to Swanage from Waterloo to spend Sunday in Swanage and admire their new railway. Leaving Waterloo on the 2.15pm express, they arrived in Swanage at 6.45 that evening. Learning of the special train, the committee in Swanage that was co-ordinating celebrations for the opening of the railway, arranged a celebration to meet the train. On arrival at the station, Mr Burt would be given an address from the townspeople thanking him for all his efforts, which had borne such wonderful results. The committee had assembled — headed by the Rev H. J. Mason, who was to give the address on Swanage station platform just after 6.00pm complete with the town band. Hundreds of people lined

the fields by the trackside between Wareham and Swanage waiting for the train. Most of the overbridges on the branch were crammed with people waiting to see the train pass. Running down the line it made a stop at Corfe Castle so that one Mr Calcraft, who boarded at Wareham, could alight. The village band played triumphantly on the platform. With the early summer sun starting to sink over Langton Matravers, the shrill whistle of the engine could be heard as the train entered the outskirts of the town. People rushed to the lineside; the platform was crammed full of people cheering and waving as the Swanage town band played on and the train crept into the platform. After profuse congratulations to Mr Burt and the board members, the Rev Mason began his speech of tribute.

After this, the party was then escorted to a large four-horse brake waiting on the station forecourt. With people cheering all about and with the town band leading, the group processed up to Purbeck House. On the evening of Tuesday 19 May, directors and officials of the LSWR travelled down to Swanage by special train and, that evening, dined with George Burt, the board of directors and guests at Purbeck House. At dinner, he gleefully spoke of the advantages that the branch line would bring to the Isle of Purbeck as a whole, and to Swanage in particular. He recounted how, as a boy, he had first visited London. It had necessitated him walking from Swanage to Poole, thence boarding a boat for Portsmouth, where he spent the night, before catching the stagecoach for London the following morning. He compared this arduous two-day expedition with the journey that the directors, officials and guests had made from London to Swanage that afternoon in a mere 4½ hours.

Wednesday 20 May 1885 was the day of the formal opening of the Swanage branch, with the first public trains and the opening of Corfe Castle and Swanage stations. The first train left Swanage at 7.20am, reaching Corfe Castle at 7.30, and departing for Worgret Junction at 7.31. Worgret Junction was passed at 7.35am with the first Swanage branch train running into the old 1847 station at Wareham at 7.45am. This day was declared a public holiday in honour of the branch's opening. George Burt's guests left Swanage by train that morning amidst much further celebration at Wareham, Corfe Castle and Swanage.

Right:
The exterior of Swanage station as built in late 1884, and viewed one evening in the mid-1930s from the present-day taxi rank. From left to right: the station master's house, booking hall, porters' lobby, toilets, station master's office, Bell & Cronin departures board, platform canopy and the W. H. Smith bookstall. The departures board, relocated in 1937 was broken up in July 1974. *Courtesy of Les Hayward*

THE SWANAGE BRANCH

3 Locomotives 1885-1972

One thing the Swanage branch did not engage in was parochialism as regards the locomotives that worked the line between 1885 and 1972. The first locomotive to run on the branch was probably a Beattie Well Tank, built in the 1860s, whilst the last to make the run down to Swanage was a Class 33 diesel-electric built in the early 1960s!

There was always something of interest in the branch's contrasting operations — from the conscientious 'M7s' to the majestic 'West Country' and 'Battle of Britain' Bulleid Pacifics, and, in the diesel era, from the plaintive whining of the 'Hampshire' diesel-electric multiple-units (DEMUs) to the seemingly unlimited power of the Brush Class 47 diesels.

Undoubtedly, the best known and most fondly remembered locomotive featured on the Swanage branch was the trusty old 'M7', which seemed to run on forever: the archetypal branch engine. First seen at Swanage in 1925, the last of them ran (amongst the last of their class still running on BR) during the first week or so of May 1964.

Although the first branch train was more than likely drawn by a Beattie 2-4-0WT, most of the branch trains until 1923 were hauled by Adams 4-4-2T locomotives. In fact, the line received one engine (No 67, later renumbered 58) brand-new from the Robert Stephenson works. With the branch entering the 20th century, the Adams tanks were joined by the Class 46

tanks ('Ironclads'). The '0522' class and 'Steamroller' 4-4-2Ts (solid bogie wheels) also ran in Purbeck. With Grouping on 1 January 1923, the LSWR was absorbed into the Southern Railway. Branch workings, increasingly hauled by Class T1 Adams 0-4-4Ts, were gradually augmented

Below:
On the glorious summer evening of Thursday 29 August 1963, Driver Jock Hapgood eases his 'M7' into Corfe Castle's up platform past the goods yard, with a train for Wareham. No 30052 had worked the branch since the previous April, moving to Bournemouth from Yeovil. She was scrapped with her other Swanage sisters at Briton Ferry, Glamorgan, in October 1964. *Rodney A. Lissenden*

Above:
One Saturday afternoon in August 1959, the usual branch train to Wareham was double-headed by 'T9' No 30729 and 'M7' No 30104. Here, the entourage leaves Swanage, the 'T9' working back to Bournemouth after arriving with a Waterloo train that morning. No 30729 was withdrawn from Exmouth Junction in March 1961 and cut up at Eastleigh; No 30104, built in 1904, was withdrawn from Bournemouth MPD in May 1961 and cut up at Eastleigh the same month.
Mervyn P. Turvey

and replaced by the 4-4-2Ts. In 1925, a number of Dugald Drummond's 'M7s' were converted for 'push-pull' use, with the altered engine weighing some 62 tons. From 1925 to 1932 they started to appear more frequently on the branch, resplendent in their handsome Maunsell green livery with black and white lining, working trains with the 'T1' 0-4-4Ts.

By the rise of Hitler in the early 1930s the 'M7s' had monopolised the branch service after having been ousted from their old haunts elsewhere on the SR with the onslaught of electrification. These marvellous little engines were to work unceasingly, plying between Wareham and Swanage, for some 39 years: from the roaring 20s through to the swinging 60s.

They toiled on through the dark days of war, through the austerity of the 1950s to the complacency of the 1960s. Even in the early 1950s the graceful 'T9s' and Dugald Drummond '700' Class 0-6-0s could still be seen scurrying along the branch — hauling anything from the branch goods or clay turn, to being station pilot at Swanage on a typically busy summer Saturday. By the 1960s, the M7s were showing their age, no longer able to take the long climb out of Swanage to Harman's Cross with ease. Their numbers dwindled steadily between 1960 and 1964, Bournemouth Motive Power Depot (MPD) being one of the last depots to use the 'M7s'. New Year's Day 1964 saw just 14 of the old girls left in

active service with BR — seven of them at Bournemouth MPD. The last 'M7s' were withdrawn in May; the last 'M7' to run down to Swanage was No 30107 around noon on Saturday 9 May 1964. The last of the Swanage 'M7s' (including No 30107) were stored in the old S&D siding at Branksome shed where Bulleid Pacifics assembled on summer Friday evenings prior to working up the S&D to Bath the following day. September 1964 saw the whole sorry assembly towed to Briton Ferry, Glamorgan, as part of the 3.20am Brighton to Salisbury freight turn. They fell to the flaming torches of scrap merchants Wards Ltd in the dying days of 1964.

As the 'M7s' came to the end of their days in Dorset, the branch played host to four 'foreign' locomotives during early 1964 — the Standard Class 3 2-6-2T — transferred down from the north of England. Brought south in order to run services after the 'M7s' were withdrawn and until certain local line closures were implemented, they were moved to Nine Elms that autumn to run empty carriage stock (ECS) workings; they were not missed by the Swanage and Bournemouth engine crews, who did not like them. The Class 2 Ivatt 2-6-2Ts first appeared on the branch early in 1963 to augment the ranks of the 'M7s', as did the Standard Class 4 2-6-4Ts in the form of No 80147 and No 80081 in August of that year. The Ivatts and the Standard tanks were well liked by

the branch crews, although running round had to be introduced at Wareham and Swanage, which the enginemen had not been used to with the old 'push-pull' 'M7s'. The Ivatt and Standard tanks were joined by the Standard '4' 2-6-0 tender engines which ran branch train services until September 1966. These latter engines first appeared at Swanage in early 1962, and one of these, No 76010, was the last 'steamer' to leave Swanage on the evening of 4 September 1966.

In May 1965 the authorities tested a Birmingham RC&W Type 3 diesel-electric locomotive (later termed a Class 33) with a view to using the class as motive power for future branch trains. Spending the day plying the branch alongside a Standard '4' tank — trains passing at Corfe Castle station — the Type 3 had two main line Bulleid coaches in tow. However, by the summer of 1966, the authorities were taking a different tack. With exactly one year of SR steam left to run, a 3-coach '3D' DEMU No 1311 (built at Eastleigh in 1962) ran the branch service on Saturday 9 July 1966. After the proposal that Swanage steam should be ousted by the end of the summer timetable, BR tried a variation on the same theme with the testing of a 2-coach 'Hampshire' DEMU No 1125 on Monday 22 August 1966, which ran the day's branch trains with an Ivatt tank.

The morning of Monday 5 September 1966 was the occasion that the first diesel branch train ran into Swanage. It had been decided that the final motive power for the Swanage branch would be the 'Hampshire' DEMU; marshalled into 2- or usually 3-coach sets; the first DEMU was unit No 1104. At this time, the autumn of 1966, the Swanage branch was the furthest west that the 'Hampshire' DEMUs worked. The advent of these brought to an end 81 years of steam traction on branch trains, although between September 1966 and June 1967, the DEMUs failed several times, necessitating the quick despatch of a worn-out Class 4 2-6-4T and two Bulleid coaches from Bournemouth, until a replacement diesel unit could be brought in from Eastleigh.

Other diesel traction ventured down the branch: during the early summer of 1967, Class 73 electro-diesels ran into Swanage in connection with the clearance of the old yard. These Class 73s, Class 33s and Class 74 electro-diesels also started to appear down the branch at this time on permanent way and ballasting trains. In

July 1967 the usual 'Hampshire' DEMU was replaced briefly by a 3-coach 'Tadpole' DEMU No 1201, composed of two 'Hastings' coaches and a single 'Hampshire' coach. During the final five years of the branch's existence, the summer months saw the usual branch trains strengthened with a 2-coach 'Hampshire' DEMU unit; Nos 1119-1122 appearing.

The final day of operation for the Swanage branch, 1 January 1972, saw 'Hampshire' DEMU No 1110 operate the usual train service. However, after the last regular timetabled train (the 21.15 from Swanage) the unit was strengthened by another 'Hampshire' DEMU No 1124, for the special last run down the branch. Nevertheless, the final train to run through Purbeck was a BR works train. On Friday 23 June 1972 Crompton Class 33 No D6580 ('push-pull' fitted) visited the branch with a steam crane and four flat wagons in tow to collect the redundant lineside huts between Swanage and Corfe Castle for use elsewhere.

Locomotives — Through Train Workings 1885-1972

From the mid-1890s, through trains to Corfe Castle and Swanage were hauled by the 'A12' 0-4-2 'Jubilees', the outside cylinder 'X2' and 'T6' 4-4-0s, together with the 'T3' and 'X6' 4-4-0s. From the turn of the century, Class 700 0-6-0s appeared on the scene; they were more powerful locomotives with smaller wheels than had hitherto been preferred. Class L11s often

appeared, piloted by 'T9s'; Class K10 Drummond 4-4-0s ran well into the 1920s. From the Depression, 'T9s' ruled the roost, often piloted by an 'M7'. Class T9s were frequently double-headed on long troop trains. During the 1930s the branch was synonymous with 'M7s' double-headed on specials: 'K10s' piloting Adams 'Seven Footers' and 'X6' 4-4-0s piloting an 'M7'. The partnership between the 'M7' and the 'T9' was famous on the line; the perfect SR scene on a rural branch line. Territorial specials and through trains via the S&D and from the GWR brought foreign locomotives to Swanage.

From 1938, the new Maunsell 'Q' class 0-6-0s worked through carriages from Wareham and Bournemouth. The initial postwar years brought through workings headed by Maunsell 'N' 2-6-0s. In the late 1940s, a through London train on a summer Saturday evening would be hauled up the branch to Wareham by a Maunsell 'Q', whence a 'T9' would take over for the run to Bournemouth. The early 1950s brought trains from the Midlands and the North, these frequently being worked by

Below:
On the cold afternoon of Friday 27 December 1963, Jack Spicer's Fireman, Keith Sloper, waits for his driver to return to No 30048's footplate, whilst engaged in shunting duties at Swanage. Minutes earlier, No 30048 had allowed Standard '4' No 80065 to depart the main platform with Driver Fred Norman in charge. Behind No 30048 is the 50ft turntable and engine shed. *C. L. Caddy*

Left:
By 1964, the 'M7s' were on their last legs. On Saturday 9 May 1964, the last working 'M7' on the Swanage branch, good old No 30107, ran the train service with Ivatt tank No 41312. Here, No 30107 makes her last journey on the branch, hauling the 12.25 Swanage-Wareham past Furzebrook Sidings. Driver Jock Hapgood had the honour of working this last trip. Coasting over the 'summit', Jock has just shut off and, to prevent blow-back, has put on the blower valve, hence the whisp of steam from No 30107's smokebox.
Anthony E. Trood

Right:
With exactly one year of Southern steam to run, the authorities tested a '3D' DEMU No 1311 on Saturday 9 July 1966, for possible use on the soon-to-be-dieselised Swanage branch. Here, No 1311 stands at Wareham's up main platform 3 after arriving from Swanage. The unit was built in 1962 at Eastleigh for the Oxted line, and was an upgraded design of the 'Hampshire' DEMUs dating from 1957.
Anthony E. Trood

Below right:
On Monday 22 August 1966, '2H' 'Hampshire' 2-coach DEMU No 1125 pauses at Corfe Castle's down platform, her 600bhp engine idling, before continuing with the 13.18 to Swanage. With Line Manager Bill Langford on board, No 1125 spent the day running the branch service with Ivatt tank No 41320, in order to evaluate the unit for use on the branch when dieselised just two weeks later.
Anthony E. Trood

Moguls from Basingstoke MPD. The Maunsell 'Rivers' reconstructed as 'U' class locomotives were frequent visitors to Swanage, as were Bulleid's 'Biscuit Barrels' (Austerity 0-6-0s built in 1942). Furthermore, Bulleid's 'West Country' and 'Battle of Britain' Pacifics started appearing on the scene from the early 1950s on Waterloo turns, and continued visiting until the summer of 1967. From 1957, these 'spam cans' became increasingly common in their rebuilt form.

At the time of the Suez Crisis in 1956, the new Standard '4' 2-6-0s appeared on local trains from Christchurch and Bournemouth, particularly on early and late turns. By the early 1960s, the Maunsell Moguls and the 'Q's were seen less frequently on Purbeck's metals, the scene being more dominated by the Standard classes, both tender and tank examples. When the Bulleid Pacifics occasionally failed or were not available, it was not unusual to see through trains hauled by a Standard tank, sometimes piloted by an 'M7'. The ECS trains down to Swanage were normally the preserve of a Standard tank or spare Pacific. The summer timetable of 1963 saw the first appearance of the Birmingham RC&W Sulzer Type 3 diesel-electric locomotives on through London trains. The decline of main line steam traction had started.

Whilst on their brief visit South, the Standard Class 3 2-6-2Ts often hauled local services to Swanage from Bournemouth and Christchurch, as well as undertaking shunting and ECS duties in relation to other through workings to Corfe Castle and Swanage. With the Waterloo to Bournemouth electrification scheme announced in September 1964, Brush Type 4 (later termed Class 47) diesel-electric locomotives appeared at Swanage by 1965 in their distinctive two-tone green livery hauling through trains for London, Southampton and Eastleigh. The last time a Brush visited Swanage was in June 1967 but, from the spring of 1967, electro-diesels appeared on the scene with the Type 3 diesel-electrics on through trains, although some through trains were still steam-hauled. The new electro-diesels (Classes 73 and 74) and the familiar Type 3s (now referred to as Class 33) were push-pull fitted to work in unison with the new 3-TC and 4-TC non-motor carriage sets introduced with the new electric service from Waterloo to Bournemouth.

Meanwhile, the final six months or so of SR steam had seen the branch visited by through steam specials, mainly hauled by a Standard tank and a Bulleid Pacific at either end of the full-length trains. On Sunday 7 May 1967, the Locomotive Club of Great Britain ran the 'Dorset Coast Express' rail tour, there being two trips down the branch. In the early afternoon, and in the rain, Standard '4' 2-6-0 No 76026 (on the Wareham end) and 'West Country' Bulleid Pacific No 34023 *Blackmore Vale* (on the Swanage end) ran down the branch. Later that afternoon, it was the turn of Standard '4' 2-6-4T No 80011 to accompany No 34023 down to Corfe Castle and Swanage. On Sunday 11 June 1967, a glorious sunny day, it was the turn of the Warwickshire Railway Society, their tour running from Birmingham. Rebuilt 'West Country' Pacific No 34004 *Yeovil* hauled the train to Wareham where Standard '4' 2-6-4T No 80146 took up the rear for the trip down the branch.

The final BR steam train to run down the branch to Swanage was organised by the RCTS for the afternoon of Sunday 18 June 1967. On this gloriously sunny summer afternoon the 12-coach train was headed by 'Battle of Britain' Bulleid Pacific No 34089 *602 Squadron* on the Swanage end with Standard tank No 80146 on the Wareham end; No 34089 had the distinction of being the last steam locomotive to be overhauled at Eastleigh works.

From Monday 10 July 1967, all Swanage through trains were hauled by 'push-pull' fitted Class 33 diesel-electrics and Class 73 and 74 electro-diesels, also 'push-pull' fitted which worked with 3-TC and 4-TC carriage stock. The first 'push-pull' fitted Class 33 diesel seen at Wareham in early 1967 was No D6535 and, in fact, the first '33' and 4-TC sets (in the all-blue livery of 1966) ran down to Swanage one fine June afternoon in 1967. The locomotive was No D6532 and was unusual in that she did not carry the usual branch headcode 98, 97 being substituted instead. Through trains continued to be thus composed through 1968 and the summer timetable of 1969.

From 1967, the very popular 10- or 12-coach excursion trains from London and the Midlands were composed of

Western Region (WR) diesel-mechanical multiple-units (DMUs) made up of 2-, 3- or 4-coach sets marshalled in any configuration. Scarcely a summer weekend went by without these long trains snaking their way down to Corfe and Swanage. They continued to run until the end of the summer timetable for 1971. In fact, several were publicised for March 1972, but had to be cancelled when the branch closed two months earlier. However, the regular timetabled through trains from London dwindled through 1969 with the result that all were withdrawn from Friday 3 October 1969. The last working of that day was hauled by Class 33 diesel No D6531 and 4-TC 'push-pull' set No 427 in the post-1967 blue and grey livery of BR. From then on, the only through workings were special excursions and ramblers' specials, often consisting of two 4-TC sets and occasionally double-headed by two Class 33s when towing three 4-TC sets. On the last day of the branch's operation, the line was visited by a 6-coach 'Hastings' DEMU No 1019 on a tour organised by the Southern Electric

Group, which ran from Blackfriars, London, to visit Dorset. This was the only DEMU that ran on the branch in the blue and grey livery.

At the opening of the branch, freight and ball clay workings were often hauled by branch locomotives with 'Black Motors', 'L11' and 'K10' 4-4-0s hauling the freight and clay workings. 'Greyhounds' were also pressed into such service. During World War 2 'Q' 0-6-0s began to be used on freight work, whereas before they had been solely used on passenger work. These continued to work the freight traffic through the 1950s and early 1960s until the spring of 1964, when the branch goods traffic was firmly in the hands of the Standard '4' 2-6-0s. Their counterparts, the Class 4 tanks, were occasionally press-ganged into goods work and it was one of these that hauled the last freight working down the branch early in October 1965.

Regarding the ball clay traffic from the sidings at Furzebrook and Norden, the late 1950s saw the appearance of Standard '4' 2-6-0s and the Bulleid Pacifics. For the final year or so of steam traction, the 10.15 departure from Poole Yard to Furzebrook was firmly in the hands of a rebuilt Bulleid Pacific, with the occasional Standard '4' 2-6-0. On light clay workings to Furzebrook, a Drewry 0-6-0 204hp shunter was employed. The last steam engine rostered for the Furzebrook turn was rebuilt 'West Country' Bulleid Pacific No 34025 *Whimple*, on Friday 30 June 1967. From the following Monday, a Class 33 diesel-electric was scheduled for this duty. The BRCW Type 3 locomotives used on the Furzebrook ball clay traffic were usually

non 'push-pull' fitted examples from Eastleigh depot. Through the 1970s the motive power was still a Class 33 with occasional visits by Class 47s.

On Saturday 3 December 1977, a special train visited Furzebrook where work had been started on the new oil terminal for the Wytch Farm on-shore oil field. The locomotive was Class 33/1 No 33114 (originally No D6532) with two 4-TC carriage sets in tow. This tour from London was arranged as a farewell to the Class 74 electro-diesels, which had worked down to Swanage in the late 1960s on through trains.

With the Wytch Farm oil terminal at Furzebrook nearing completion, the first locomotive to enter the terminal was Class 47 No 47369 light engine. The first oil train to the terminal was hauled by Class 47 No 47268 on a practice-familiarisation run on Tuesday 25 July 1978. The terminal formally received its first oil train on Friday 15 December 1978. Since then, Class 47s (the old Brush Type 4s) have held a monopoly over the oil trains after an initial period when the trains were double-headed with Class 33s. There have also been rare glimpses of Class 50 and 56 diesels at the terminal. However, despite the old stub of the Swanage branch booming with Wytch Farm oil trains, the ball clay traffic had dwindled steadily since 1980. Indeed, by 1983 the traffic was so small that it was catered for by the Wool freight working (for the Bovington Ministry of Defence camp) which made a detour up the branch, invariably hauled by a Class 33, until the clay traffic ended in early 1984.

Below:

Class 47s (then known as Brush Type 4s) first worked to Swanage from 1965. After the branch was closed they reappeared in the early 1980s on bulk oil trains to Furzebrook, and the SR's railhead for the Wytch Farm on-shore oil field. Built opposite the clay works of ECC in 1978, Class 47 No 47435 (Gateshead shed) reverses 10 empty 100-tonne bogie oil tankers into the terminal on the bitterly cold morning of Tuesday 25 February 1986. The 10 loaded tankers are at the far end of the main line, waiting to be hauled to Fawley. *Andrew P. M. Wright*

THE SWANAGE BRANCH

4 Rundown and closure 1962-72

The 1962 Transport Act abolished the old Transport Commission, placing the responsibility for railway administration on BR. This 'paved the way for a drastic streamlining of the industry' and produced the infamous *Report on the Railways* by the Board's Dr Richard Beeching, a refugee from ICI, published on Wednesday 27 March 1963. Although the Report did not affect or mention the main Bournemouth to Weymouth line with the feeder to Swanage, the branch felt the first icy death-grip of Beeching in late August 1962. It was announced that from the start of the winter timetable on Monday 10 September, Corfe Castle and Swanage would lose their two through carriages on the 'Royal Wessex' train, passengers having to change trains at Wareham.

With the start of the winter 1963 timetable, Sunday branch trains were suspended; for the next nine years Sunday trains would only run during the summer timetable. During this same year the authorities tried to close the goods yards at Swanage and Corfe Castle, and to withdraw the goods service, Purbeck freight being concentrated on Wareham. However, both individuals and Purbeck councils alike protested vociferously, delaying the closures until Monday 4 October 1965, after the branch goods service had been run down for several years. Corfe Castle lost its Station Master in 1963, the last one being Mr Smith who moved on to Broadstone, whilst Swanage's last Station Master, Harry Newman, had moved on by June 1966 to Brockenhurst and then Winchester.

Swanage and Corfe Castle stations then came under a Line Manager at Wareham, Mr Bill Langford. In mid-August 1966 he

Below:
The last weekend of branch steam traction at Corfe. Below the castle on the morning of Saturday 3 September 1966, No 80134 prepares to leave with the 09.20 Swanage-Wareham. At the station, No 80134 had passed Ivatt tank No 41316 running light engine to Swanage. *C. L. Caddy*

Right:
Swanage station and yard from Northbrook Road bridge on Saturday 3 September 1966. With Standard '4' No 80138 in the yard's siding No 4 (sidings 5 and 6 having been lifted during June 1966), No 34004 *Yeovil* waits for the 10.47 from Wareham to draw into the bay platform before departing with the 11.20 to Waterloo. *C. L. Caddy*

Below:
Standard '4' 2-6-0 No 76010 departs Swanage on the evening of Sunday 4 September 1966, at the end of the last day of Swanage branch steam. Behind No 76010 is the bay platform and station master's house. The curved roofed hut by the yard was the station foreman's office. *Anthony E. Trood*

received a letter from the Divisional Manager, informing him that from Monday 5 September 1966 the branch service would be run by a 'Hampshire' DEMU, the timetable being changed accordingly, so that one unit could run the daily service. He also told Mr Langford that in June it had been recommended the branch should be closed and Corfe Castle and Swanage stations abandoned, with a stopblock set up at Furzebrook. The news of the new traction and timetable for the branch was officially announced by the SR on Wednesday 31 August 1966. Trains would run hourly between 07.00 and 21.00 in either direction. By this time, the station staff at Corfe Castle consisted of two Signalmen, Bob Inman and a relief, Leading Porter/Signalman Bob Richards (who also worked in the booking office), and a porter. As for Swanage, the staff

there was made up of two Signalmen, Arthur Galton and Jimmy Hunt, Station Master Harry Newman, Station Foreman Jack Cannons, a senior parcels porter, and three Porters, Bill 'Taffy' Hazell, George Sims and Tom Tetley, the latter two being Porter/Shunters at the station. The two Booking Clerks were Maurice Walton and Bryan Green.

The summer of 1966 saw the last full train service run under steam traction, trains passing at Corfe Castle. The end of the summer timetable on the evening of Sunday 4 September 1966, finally brought to an end an era of services such as through trains to Salisbury, Alton and Eastleigh. On this fine evening, Swanage's engine shed was closed for good, having been a sub-shed of Bournemouth MPD.

Sunday 4 September 1966 was the last day of Swanage branch steam traction.

Standard '4' 2-6-0 No 76010 was rostered to work the branch service for the whole day. After working the branch on the previous Saturday evening, she spent the night in the Swanage engine shed, the last locomotive to do so before it closed. Three sets of engine crews manned No 76010 through the day: the first set of Swanage men signed on at 08.43. No 76010 was eased out of the engine shed and across the turntable at 09.33 before working the first train of the day, the 10.03 to Wareham. The second Swanage crew relieved the first at Swanage at 14.15, working the branch until 19.40 when they were relieved by a Bournemouth crew at Wareham, who then worked the 19.44 down branch train. The final passenger train from Swanage was the 20.14 with Bournemouth MPD's Johnny Walker driving. There were long hoots from No 76010's whistle and cracks from

Above:

The first day of diesel traction on the Swanage branch. On the blustery afternoon of Monday 5 September 1966, 3-coach 'Hampshire' DEMU No 1104 accelerates away from Swanage's platform 1 past the signalbox, with the 16.20 to Corfe Castle and Wareham. Motor coaches park on the old cattle dock in the yard, whilst a rake of Bulleid coaches stands in siding No 4, having arrived from Waterloo behind steam. *John H. Bird*

Left:

A desolate scene at Swanage on Monday 26 June 1967, in between visits from 3-coach 'Hampshire' DEMU No 1127, viewed through the Northbrook bridge from the coaling dock and water tower. The station is a railway in limbo, displaying all the vestiges of the past steam era, but now in modern diesel days awaiting the demolition gang. The signalbox had been closed just 20 days earlier. Six months later all this would be gone.
George M. Moon

detonators on the track as Swanage's last steamer departed. Many locals turned out early to watch her leave. However, many missed this last trip, a railway official leaking the fact that No 76010 would leave Swanage 15min late; in actual fact she left on time. Detonators were also placed on the track at Corfe Castle, and many people travelled on the train to Corfe Castle and Wareham. One of its passengers was Mr Sidney Smith, who had first left Swanage by train before World War 1 when he attended Skuse's School at Wareham. No 76010's very last trip up the Swanage branch was light engine at 21.55, reaching Bournemouth MPD at 22.50. This was also No 76010's last trip for, after being attached to Bournemouth since the previous October and hauling the last steam working through Purbeck to Corfe Castle and Swanage, she was withdrawn,

stored at Eastleigh and cut up in Newport, South Wales, in March 1967.

Monday 5 September 1966 brought a new era to the Swanage branch and accelerated the progress of running down prior to closure. A new timetable was brought in and, by the end of steam traction on the main line on Monday 10 July 1967, just one DEMU worked between Wareham and Swanage. This necessitated tight turnaround times at both ends. Previously in June, notice had been given to the staff at Swanage informing them that from 10 July the staff would be cut to just two. One of the Booking Clerks, Bryan Green, had left the service of BR the previous March, as had Signalmen Jimmy Hunt and Bob Inman. However, the railwaymen were quick to point out to the Area Manager, Mr Harold Ward, that these cuts would coincide with the branch's

busiest time. Rather embarrassed, the authorities withdrew the notice, making it clear, however, that the staff cuts at Swanage would be implemented later. These fell that September.

The postwar years witnessed considerable contraction in the numbers of gangers employed to maintain the branch track. Between the wars, the branch had been divided into six lengths with each length being maintained by a group of gangers. Gradually though, duties were amalgamated and manning levels reduced, so that by the early 1960s the entire branch was maintained by two six-men gangs: one based at Corfe Castle which tended the Worgret Junction to Corfe section, and the other at Swanage, which tended the Corfe to Swanage section of the branch. With the end of branch steam, track maintenance costs dropped and the profusion of tracks at Swanage became obsolete. Thus, on Monday 24 April 1967, the two six-men gangs at Corfe Castle and Swanage were disbanded. From this date, the whole branch was maintained by a 'mobile' gang based at Wareham; in 1971 this numbered 11 railwaymen.

Meanwhile, the rationalisation of the branch timetable was causing much concern to Purbeck's populace. The school trains had been retimed so that children did not have enough time to travel to school from the station and vice versa. All Purbeck's councils supported these parental objections and, as the 1960s came to an end, the chorus of criticism against BR's actions grew ever louder.

On Wednesday 18 October 1967, Purbeck people were shocked to read notices in *The Times* and the *Daily Telegraph* in which BR indicated that they intended to print a formal public notice of their proposal to close the Swanage branch line. On Wednesday 6 December 1967, as Swanage's surplus track was being lifted, BR formally announced that they intended to close the branch line on Monday 9 September 1968. The Transport Users' Consultative Committee (TUCC) hearing, set up with the 1962 Transport Act, was held at the Mowlem Theatre, Swanage, (within sight of the station), on Tuesday 14 May 1968. The theatre was packed and the Committee heard hundreds of objections from residents, parish councils, local authorities and Dorset County Council as to why the branch should not close. By 10 August their verdict had been leaked: the TUCC supported Purbeck against the closure.

By this time the station staff at Swanage had been cut to four: one Booking Clerk, Maurice Walton; two Porters, Bill 'Taffy' Hazell and George Sims; and a Station Foreman, Jack Cannons. Early January 1969 brought further rumours that the branch would close despite the massive public feeling in Purbeck. By the end of the month, the Transport Minister Richard Marsh announced that the Swanage branch line would close on Monday 6 October 1969. This in turn was delayed until Monday 5 January 1970, local authorities objecting to the provision of replacement bus services. Sadly, Jack Cannons, Station Foreman at Swanage since 1963, was made redundant by BR on Monday 6 October 1969. He soon revealed that BR had let the line 'go to pot' and described their claim that the branch lost some £79,000 during 1968 as 'bunkum'. By the summer of 1969, all but one of the through trains to London from Swanage had been withdrawn. BR had introduced special fares on through London trains, but they had built in prohibitive restrictions such as only travelling when there were slow trains. At the time Mr Cannons left, the last London train had departed Swanage, the rail service from then on being purely a branch affair with passengers having to change at Wareham for main line trains. The deadline of 5 January 1970 came and went. The next provisional closure date was to be Saturday 2 May; the branch timetable was again altered causing further protests. Locals took the sight of work being done on the branch track as a sign that the line had been reprieved. Others thought this to be a cunning attempt to boost the alleged losses of the Swanage branch.

With Dorset County Council and the Purbeck councils still opposing the replacement bus service licences, BR announced on Monday 2 February 1970 that the branch would not close in April as planned, but would continue until September 1970. This was later extended to the end of that year and, in early February 1971, until the end of the following summer season. Despite these depressing times, with the timetable for 1971 pointing out that the branch service could be withdrawn at any time, a taste of the good old days returned in April 1971. The three surviving members of staff at Swanage station were awarded third prize in the SR best-kept station competition. One of the porters, Bill 'Taffy' Hazell, travelled to London to receive the award from the SR's Divisional Manager, S. L. Edwards. The certificate was framed and placed, with the many others the station had received in the postwar years, in the booking hall. Finally, on Saturday 6 November 1971, BR gave another date for the closure of the Swanage branch. This time there was to be no reprieve: the branch would close on the morning of Monday 3 January 1972; there being no winter Sunday service, the final trains in the Isle of Purbeck would run on the previous Saturday, New Year's Day.

On Saturday 1 January 1972, the appointed day arrived for the last trains to run on the first day of the Swanage branch's 87th year of operation. Typically, perhaps, the day was dismal and overcast. Many enthusiasts came to Purbeck to

Below:
Sulzer power amongst the weeds at Corfe Castle. On the evening of Thursday 7 August 1969, Class 33 No D6538 and 4-TC set No 427, rumble into the weed-ridden station loop with the 18.14 Swanage-Bournemouth working; this was the return working off the 15.30 from Waterloo. This picture, taken from the abandoned end-loading dock, shows the goods yard partially lifted deep amongst the weeds. L. G. Stockley's coal yard is to the right. *John Scrace*

Right:
Swanage station's Foreman, Jack Cannons, was made redundant by BR on Monday 6 October 1969, after working at Swanage since 1963. Here, at his retirement party at the Railway Hotel, Swanage, Jack is presented with a farewell present by the Line Manager Bill Langford, who himself retired in November 1977. From left to right: Swanage Porter Bill 'Taffy' Hazell, Corfe Signalman Bob Richards, Mrs Cannons, Mrs Richards, Jack Cannons, Wareham Shunter Paddy Mulqueen, Swanage Porter George Sims, Wareham Booking Clerk Rex Spinney, Bill Langford, Swanage Booking Clerk Maurice Walton, and Harold Cook, owner of the station bookstall at Swanage. Sadly, George Sims died in the autumn of 1972 after being made redundant from the branch line that was his life.
Courtesy of W. R. Hazell

Above:
Swanage station showing all the faceless anonymity of BR with 3-coach 'Hampshire' DEMU No 1129 departing a 'rationalised' station for Corfe Castle and Wareham on Sunday 1 June 1969. Left with just a single line, and with the signalbox, bay track and sidings gone, Swanage station was a dismembered relic of former days. The station master's allotment in the foreground has long been overgrown.
George M. Moon

Right:
The Swanage branch track gang at Corfe Castle station on Christmas Eve 1971, after a hard day's work on the doomed branch line. Standing, left to right: Stan Smith, Edwin 'Ted' Talbot, Eddy Bird, Cyril Tilly and Charlie Bird. Seated, left to right: John Coogan (the gang's driver), Arthur Stockley, Tom Stockley, Ken Ridout and Tom Biles. The eleventh member of the gang, Tony Trood, was 'otherwise engaged'. *Anthony E. Trood*

Left:
On the Swanage branch's last day, Saturday 1 January 1972, 3-coach 'Hampshire' DEMU No 1110 waits under the grimy canopy, last painted in 1954, to form the next train to Corfe. The bay track and run-round loop were lifted in November 1967. With Porter Bill 'Taffy' Hazell blowing the whistle to send the last train off that night, few thought Swanage would ever see a train again.
John R. Coleman

Bottom:
At Wareham's platform 3, after returning from Swanage and Corfe Castle with the last train, Driver Johnny Walker shakes hands with the Mayor of Wareham, Councillor Eric Mole. Between them are Line Manager for the branch, Bill Langford, and Mrs Mole. *Arthur Grant*

the track. The train pulled into a mournful Corfe Castle station for the last time at 22.24 before arriving at Wareham's up main platform 3 at 22.40. The train then returned, stopping at all stations to Bournemouth, before returning to Eastleigh depot.

As with the branch's last steam working, this last train of all was driven by Johnny Walker of Bournemouth who was only weeks away from retirement himself. He had known the branch well, regularly driving it in the steam and diesel days. As well as driving the last steamer out of Swanage in September 1966, he had driven 'Merchant Navy' No 35028 *Clan Line* on one of the last trains up the S&D line on Sunday 6 March 1966.

There had been all kinds of threats against the last train to run to Corfe Castle and Swanage. People were going to chain themselves to the track and it was leaked that 'the boys from the Lazy C Ranch', Creech Bottom, were going to hold up the train at the Creech Bottom crossing on horseback and dressed in 'Wild West' costume. However, Line Manager Bill Langford called in the police. The last train had Railway Police on board with County Police at the farm crossings, deterring any would-be kidnappers. In the event, the assembled TV crews and photographers, equipped with arc-lights, were disappointed as the last trip went without incident.

On this last day at Corfe Castle station, the small signalbox on the up platform was manned by Arthur Galton from 05.45 to 13.45, with Bob Richards taking over as Corfe's last signalman from 13.45 until 23.00. The last train left the Corfe Castle to Worgret Junction block section at 22.37, the last to do so, with the closing signals between Corfe and Worgret Junction boxes taking place at 23.00. Bob Richards then signed off duty, locked the small signalbox and left the station for the last time.

Officially, the Swanage branch line of BR closed to passenger traffic at 07.08 on the morning of Monday 3 January 1972. This was the time that the first train of the day would have passed Worgret Junction signalbox en route for Corfe and Swanage, had closure not taken place.

watch and ride on the last trains: 3-coach 'Hampshire' DEMU No 1110 being rostered to spend the day plying between Wareham, Corfe Castle and Swanage. As well as the usual service, the branch was visited by a special train from London. This railtour, the 'Purbeck Piper', organised by the Southern Electric Group, departed Blackfriars at 09.28, pulling into Corfe Castle at 17.28; the 6-coach 'Hastings' DEMU No 1019 then waited at the down platform for the 17.32 from Swanage to arrive in the loop. Departing at 17.44, the special train pulled into Swanage at 17.53. Departing the almost derelict terminus at 17.58 bound for Victoria, the train arrived at Corfe Castle at 18.10 (passing the 18.00 from Wareham) before departing past the castle at 18.13 bound for Wareham and London.

After the regular train service to Swanage had ceased on New Year's Day 1972, with the 21.15 arriving at Wareham's north bay platform 4, 3-coach 'Hampshire' DEMU No 1110 was strengthened with

3-coach 'Hampshire' DEMU No 1124 on the Swanage end for the special last trip down to Corfe Castle and Swanage. Understandably, this last train was boycotted by councillors from Swanage UDC and the Wareham and Purbeck RDC. The Mayor of Wareham, Councillor Eric Mole, who travelled on the train with other borough councillors said, 'This will in no way be an event which anyone here will be celebrating. It will be more of a requiem'.

The special train, with 500 passengers aboard who had each paid 50p for the commemorative ticket, left Wareham's south bay platform 1 at 21.45, reaching Corfe Castle at 22.00 and Swanage at 22.10. A long-time member of staff who was a real character, Bill 'Taffy' Hazell, had the honour of blowing the whistle and waving off the last train from Swanage. It pulled away from the packed platforms at 22.15 on this cold, dark night, to the funereal accompaniment of the hissing gas lamps, which vaguely illuminated the station, and cracks from the detonators on

THE SWANAGE BRANCH

5   Tracklifting and decay 1972-76

With the Swanage branch closing to passenger traffic on the morning of Monday 3 January 1972, the statutory 6-month 'limbo' period ensued before BR could tear up the track and recover its assets. Apart from the signals at Corfe Castle being stripped of their enamel arms, the line remained intact. Many locals took this opportunity to walk the silent tracks before they were lifted. Between January and July 1972, the Swanage Railway Society fought tenaciously to stop the branch track from being hurriedly lifted. Bull's taxi company of Swanage were concerned that the redevelopment of the station site would oust them from the only suitable rank in the town. In February, it was announced that a plan to develop the terminus station site for a shop and hotel complex was to go ahead. Swanage residents and councillors protested. It also became known that Dorset County Council planned to demolish the dangerous

Victoria Avenue road bridge, realign the road and also acquire the railway trackbed through Corfe Castle for a much-awaited Corfe bypass.

In late April 1972, the war-weary Isle of Purbeck Preservation Group, founded in 1969, officially gave up their fight to buy and operate the branch line. British Rail wanted £115,000 for the seven miles of trackbed and heavily worn track between Swanage and Furzebrook, as well as an extra £11,500 for the loss of interest on the scrap value of the track.

On the morning of Friday 23 June 1972, just nine days before tracklifting operations were scheduled to begin, Class 33 locomotive No D6580 ran down the branch with a works train to collect the redundant concrete lineside huts between Corfe Castle and Swanage for re-use on the main Bournemouth to Weymouth line between Holton Heath and Wool. This train, which originated from Eastleigh, had in tow a SR

brake van, four flat wagons, SR travelling steam crane No D5414, with SR utility van trailing. Wareham's 'mobile' track gang, which had maintained the rusting branch track from Monday 24 April 1967 until six months previously, joined the train at Corfe station for the day's work. In charge of this work was Sub-Inspector, the late Arthur Yetman, of Blandford Forum, who was attached to the Weymouth Permanent Way Depot. The four huts collected were at Swanage station, Herston, New Barn

Below:
The last train of all, a works train, ran down the Swanage branch on Friday 23 June 1972. Class 33 No D6580, with steam crane and flat wagons, runs into Corfe station from Wareham past the gaunt castle and stripped up starter signal, just nine days before tracklifting operations were scheduled to commence. *Anthony E. Trood*

bridge and Corfe Castle station, with No D6580 running round its train, after each hut had been recovered, via the Corfe loop. The train finally returned with its unusual load to Wareham late that afternoon. All that remained was for the branch to be lifted.

On Saturday 1 July 1972, exactly six months to the day after the last train ran, the Swanage Railway Society announced their plans to buy the branch line and run an amenity service for Purbeck's population, subsidised by steam trains during the tourist season. Extra halts would be installed at Worgret (for the large comprehensive school serving Purbeck), Blue Pool (Furzebrook), Harman's Cross and Herston, so that as many people as possible could benefit from the railway. The Society would negotiate with BR for 'running rights' over their tracks into Wareham station.

The next day, BR was due to commence tracklifting operations. This was delayed, however, after the Swanage Railway Society agreed to pay the interest on the scrap value of the track, but only after an independent valuation of the track, which was estimated to be worth only £50,000. However, on the bright morning of Monday 10 July 1972, tracklifting operations began at Corfe Castle station, watched by BR area officials. BR had awarded the contract to Eagre & Co of Scunthorpe, whose foreman on this job, David Meeham, said, 'British Rail asked us to start as quickly as we could. We will have it lifted within five weeks'. Telegrams were immediately sent to the Minister of the Environment, Peter Walker, and Richard Marsh, Chairman of the British Railways Board, by the Swanage Railway Society and the Swanage UDC asking them to intervene and stop the lifting. The Swanage Railway Society complained that they had 'been sold down the river by British Rail' who had promised informally that lifting would not start whilst negotiations were in progress. South Dorset Member of Parliament, Evelyn King, said the following day, 'I'm very angry about this. A British Rail official assured me at 5.30pm yesterday that no lifting had taken place. I have been misinformed'.

The residents of Corfe Castle were none too pleased either. One resident, who lived within sight of the station, clearly remembers on that fateful Monday Richard Marsh, in a local television interview, state categorically that lifting on the branch would not start whilst, through the window, Eagre & Co could be seen and heard at work tearing up the track!

After this ceremonial start at Corfe Castle, lifting started at Swanage, the gang working up the branch. By Monday 17 July, the track was dismantled past Herston and, by the 24th, past Haycraft's Lane overbridge at Harman's Cross. By the end of that hot July, the gang had reached Afflington, and by the close of the first week of August work was well in hand dismantling the Corfe Castle passing loop, the rails being craned on to flat wagons for

later removal by a Class 33 diesel up the line. Three open wagons were also provided for other scrap such as chairs, keys and bolts. By Monday 14 August, the track had been lifted past Eldon's siding at Norden and the Woodpecker cutting. With the end of that sixth week, the track was lifted past the Norden curve and the A351 Catseye bridge to a point about half a mile from Furzebrook Sidings in the Corfe direction. Here, amongst the pine trees, a stop block was erected and this is now the furthest the branch penetrates the Isle of Purbeck.

Regarding the speedy tracklifting during that hot summer of 1972, British Road Services were contracted to carry the scrap away, with farm tractors used to haul the cut rails along the sleepers to the articulated lorries. The sleepers were uprooted from the ballast using JCB mechanical diggers. A good deal of the wooden sleepers were sold to Mr Hallett of Ridge, whilst the concrete sleepers were retained by BR for future use on the main line and transported to Wareham station for storage. These were piled high opposite the signalbox on the site of the station master's house, but were found to be unsuitable for re-use and sold to the Severn Valley Railway in March 1978. It is rather ironic that some of the Swanage Railway's first track, laid in the very early days of

1977 and 1978, was laid on old Swanage branch sleepers purchased from Mr Hallett!

Access for the plant and equipment used in the tracklifting was via the farm crossings closest to the railhead. It was not, however, an easy task as the farm tracks were narrow and winding. Many of the articulated lorries carrying large quantities of redundant sleepers and rails became stuck in the drainage ditches and culverts.

Despite the speedy lifting of the branch track during the summer, the Swanage Railway Society continued fighting to at least limit the damage being done. They persuaded BR to leave the ballast on the lifted section, as well as the signal posts at Corfe Castle and other sundry buildings still remaining at Swanage, all of which would be most useful when the line was rebuilt. BR also instructed their contractors, Eagre & Co, to stop tracklifting at a point ½-mile short of that originally agreed at Furzebrook, thus leaving a very useful spur on which could be stored the Swanage Railway Society's track relaying train when the branch was rebuilt.

On the afternoon of Saturday 29 July 1972, the Swanage Railway Society arranged a 'sit-down' protest by 16 members on the partially dismantled track at New Barn; the contractors, however, treated it as a joke. With the branch track

lifted completely by mid-August and Nature making a remorseless comeback, Dorset County Council commenced negotiations with BR over the purchase of the redundant trackbed between Catseye bridge, Norden, and the Northbrook Road bridge, Swanage.

In March 1974, Swanage Town Council purchased the station site at Swanage from BR, deciding not to let the land to the Swanage Railway Society, who were concerned at the rapid deterioration of the station buildings. In July of that year the Council demolished the western end of the

Left:
On the fine morning of Monday 10 July 1972, tracklifting began at Corfe Castle station, watched by BR area officials. This dramatic view shows one of Eagre & Co's workmen at work that afternoon, cutting up the old point treadle on the Swanage end of the Corfe passing loop. In the distance is the desolate station with the castle towering above. *Arthur Grant*

Above:
Corfe Castle station looking towards Wareham in the first week of August 1972. By this time the contractors lifting the Swanage branch track, Eagre & Co of Scunthorpe, were dismantling the passing loop, the scrap being thrown on to the platform. All that remains is for the JCBs and lorries to uproot and collect the sleepers. *Robert J. Richards*

Right:
Corfe Castle station on the afternoon of Tuesday 9 April 1985, in the branch's centenary year, and 13 years after the tracks were lifted. With the Norman Castle dominating the village, the station awaits the Swanage Railway Project's track relaying train. To the left, behind the undergrowth, is the old end-loading dock and goods shed. In 1983, the station buildings were leased to Eastpoint Ltd, an electronics company; one of its directors, Les Hayward, has restored them to their former glory. *Andrew P. M. Wright*

long station platform, as well as the old air-raid shelter by the site of the signalbox, the station foreman's office and the old wagon weighbridge in the yard. The station canopy, built in 1938, was stripped of its lead and glass leaving a rusty skeleton. The Bell & Cronin indicator board was broken up, as were the small lamp and gas rooms by the site of the buffer stops, removed two years previously. The trackbed by the main platform was infilled with rubble from the bulldozed platform. The flattened platform now formed part of an enlarged car and bus park.

Before the summer of 1974 was out, coaches and Hants & Dorset double-deck buses, which replaced the old train service, parked across the site where, just over two years previously, the last whining DEMU had left the almost derelict station; where, a mere eight years before, 'West Country' Pacifics had simmered and Class 47s had throbbed, waiting to haul packed through trains to Waterloo. Across in the wind-swept yard, the rakes of green carriages were replaced by lines of cars parked there for the day.

In March 1975, the new Swanage fire station was formally opened on the site of a coal merchant's and old stone cutters' huts on the south side of the station yard. Meanwhile, at Corfe Castle station, the Royal British Legion still leased the booking hall (as they had done ever since July 1969) but by 1976, Jack Cannons, Swanage station's Foreman until October 1969, had moved out of the station and out of Dorset. He had witnessed the branch wither and die, with the track being torn up right outside his kitchen window. However, despite decay and sprawling undergrowth all round, he always kept his windowboxes and hanging baskets pristinely stocked with flowers, — right up to the end. Thus by 1976, Corfe Castle's station master's house was boarded up, like Swanage station four years before, and left to face an uncertain future.

THE SWANAGE BRANCH

6 The Phoenix Rises –
the Swanage Railway Project, 1975-1993

'It's like the Channel Tunnel project. You'll never see it in this century or ever — a lot of rubbish, all of it,' sneered a dismissive Swanage resident in April 1975, after being asked about the chances of the branch railway ever coming back to life; as the Victorian station lay boarded up and close to being demolished.

Eighteen years later in 1993, the Swanage Railway was firmly back on the Dorset scene — with nearly six miles of track relaid to within half a mile of the BR network at Furzebrook. A few yards of hand-laid track have turned into a business poised to achieve a £1 million annual turnover, passenger figures for just three miles of line between Swanage and Harman's Cross exceeding 100,000 people a year and a nationwide — indeed worldwide — membership of over 2,500 people from Swanage to Sydney and San Francisco.

Since the first train — a small diesel shunter and a half-painted 1940s Bulleid carriage — ran a few yards in 1979 nearly one million people have been carried five million miles on the relaid Purbeck Line. With the earning of practical and moral support of BR and local authorities, the Swanage Railway has come of age. A seemingly hopeless dream hatched in a rash moment of exuberance on a lazy summer day in 1972 has become reality.

Back in July 1975 — the time of the British referendum on whether the country should stay in Europe — the situation was very different. The still elegant Victorian station buildings were boarded up, marooned in a sea of weed-infested ballast, desolation and decay. It seemed that no one

wanted to know about a rebuilt Swanage Railway. Volunteers were banging their heads against a brick wall — or were they?

The Swanage Railway Project started at Corfe Castle on a warm summer day in May 1972 when London railway enthusiast and psychology student Andrew Goltz visited the newly abandoned station. Walking along the rusting and weed-clogged tracks just weeks before they were ripped up for scrap, he decided there and then to try and save the branch line.

After three years of near constant campaigning by the newly-formed Swanage Railway Society, Dorset County Council agreed to the six and a half miles of disused trackbed between the stub of the old BR line at Furzebrook and the Northbrook Road bridge at Swanage station being used as a railway. It was not until a referendum among Swanage people in July 1975, revealed that a massive 83% wanted the trains back that the town council agreed to lease the boarded-up station buildings to the Society for just one year — to prove themselves — but with no track laying allowed.

The first tangible evidence that railway volunteers really meant business was when the Southern Steam Trust (formed in 1974 with the now absorbed Swanage to Wareham Railway Group) bought its first ex-BR main line steam locomotive, Standard Class 4 2-6-4T No 80078 from Barry scrapyard.

At the same time, the Society moved into the station goods shed at Swanage which was to become an important focus for locomotive and carriage restoration work. In February 1976, jubilant volunteers gained entry to the boarded-up station master's house and booking office to start work on halting the rapid deterioration and providing a base for the project.

A bombshell that left volunteers reeling was dropped in the spring of 1977 when the town council revealed it wanted to build a health centre on part of the old goods yard at Swanage. It was small consolation when the Society was told it could start to lay a few yards of track. Seven miles up the line at Furzebrook, work was close to completion on a rail terminal to handle crude oil from Europe's largest on-shore oil field at

Right:
In her original air-smoothed casing, unrebuilt 'Battle of Britain' class Bulleid Pacific No 34072 *257 Squadron* of 1948 waits to leave Swanage with a train for Harman's Cross on Sunday 3 February 1991.
Andrew P. M. Wright

Left:
A red letter day for the Swanage Railway was the arrival on a 10-year loan from the National Railway Museum, York, of LSWR Dugald Drummond 'T9' class 4-4-0 No 120 in early 1991. Built at Nine Elms in 1899, No 120 first operated in Dorset during World War 1 — making her last trip in the county during 1960. No 120's crew narrowly escaped death after the loco was attacked by two Luftwaffe fighters at Wool station on Saturday 28 November 1942. Withdrawn by BR in 1960, No 30120 knocked up over two million miles. Here the veteran backs onto her train — and GWR '56xx' class 0-6-2T No 5619 of 1925 from Telford — at Swanage on Friday 29 March 1991.
Andrew P. M. Wright

Wytch Farm. Society volunteers took consolation that the development would ensure the remaining three miles of the branch would not be lifted.

By November 1977, Swanage Town Council had abandoned its plans for a health centre on railway land and issued a positive statement of intent about the Society's long-term aims of a link up with BR near Wareham. More track laying was allowed in 1978 with the 1938 extended station canopy at Swanage fully restored, thanks to a government employment scheme.

With Dorset County Council producing its draft passenger transport plan which included a rebuilt Swanage Railway, the Society submitted its plan for a park and ride system for Purbeck to relieve horrific seasonal traffic jams. A similar scheme between BR and local authorities in St Ives, Cornwall, had been and still is highly successful.

It was a historic day in February 1979, when volunteers formed the Swanage Railway Company with the objectives of buying the trackbed and stations along the old branch and resurrecting an all-year amenity train service for local people, supplemented by steam trains during the tourist seasons.

Tuesday 15 May 1979 saw the county council finally agree to the railway project

laying track and operating a one-mile service to Herston. The first passenger train at Swanage since 1 January 1972 — a 250hp 0-4-0 Fowler diesel shunter *May* and a half-painted Bulleid carriage — left a temporary scaffolding platform under Northbrook Road bridge in August 1979. Steam traction began a few weeks later with Andrew Barclay 0-4-0ST *Richard Trevithick*. It may have only been a 200yd journey with tickets just 10p, but to the volunteers it seemed the world. They had started.

The Swanage Railway has always had to balance the need to run revenue-earning trains and the task of rebuilding the Purbeck Line. With the first fledgling trains running, volunteers started to relay the tracks from Swanage — heading for the one-mile point at Herston and the site of a new halt that officially received its first train on Good Friday, 1984.

Further progress came when Dorset County Council agreed that the Swanage Railway should be granted a lease of the trackbed as far as Harman's Cross, three miles from Swanage and just two from

Corfe Castle — on Thursday 26 February 1981. The laying of track beyond Herston was speeded up in 1984 with a 1947 Southern Railway diesel-electric crane which could lay track in 60ft panels instead of the volunteers laboriously working by hand. The tracks reached the proposed Harman's Cross station — sporting two six-coach platforms which never existed in BR days — in February 1988.

A spectre that has hung over the Swanage Railway for much of its history has been the prospect of the trackbed through Corfe Castle being used for a bypass, first pegged out in 1933. The nightmare evaporated on Thursday 26 July 1986, when county councillors voted that railway land should not be used — a route skirting the east of the village chosen instead.

Harman's Cross station — the first wholly new station to be built in Dorset in over half a century — was formally opened on Saturday 4 March 1989, by Gordon Pettitt, General Manager of BR's Southern Region. It was certainly a good year for the Swanage Railway, with praise for the volunteers' efforts coming from Chris Green, then the high-powered director of BR Network SouthEast, later to move to BR Inter-City. 'You are performing miracles as you narrow the gap between Harman's Cross and Furzebrook,' he wrote after a visit to Swanage with NSE Planning & Investment Manager John Norman on Saturday

Right:
An inspiring sight which most local people — and some railway enthusiasts — never thought they would ever see. Swanage Railway volunteers relay the passing loop and headshunt point for the goods yard at a rapidly re-emerging Corfe Castle station on Thursday 16 April 1992. On the track relaying train is ex-BR Class 08 0-6-0 diesel shunter D3591 (ex-TOPS No 08476) built at Crewe in 1958 and acquired in 1986 to power permanent way trains 'up the bank' to Harman's Cross. During the 1970s and 1980s Corfe's abandoned Victorian station came close to being flattened for a bypass.
Andrew P. M. Wright

Left:

Newly restored 'Yankee Tank' 0-6-0T No 30075 shunts a goods train in Swanage station run-round loop on Saturday 19 September 1992. Originally No 62 669, it was built in Yugoslavia during 1960 to the wartime American design and completed just 25,000 miles before being withdrawn and then rescued just hours before Slovenia declared independence with the start of the bitter civil war. American 'lend-lease' Yankee Tanks ran in southern England before D-Day 1944, and accompanied invading forces into Europe. In 1947, 14 were purchased by the Southern Railway some of which survived until the end of steam in 1967.
Andrew P. M. Wright

Below left:

The typical branch line scene at Swanage station. Edwardian 'M7' class 0-4-4T No 30053 of 1905 simmers in the hot summer sun before departing with the 15.40 for Herston and Harman's Cross on Sunday 19 July 1992. Purchased from Steamtown, USA, in July 1986 for just £24,000, the 1897-Dugald Drummond designed No 30053 — which last left Swanage with a train for Wareham in April 1964 — was brought home to Dorset in April 1987. It took more than £100,000 and four years of restoration work by the Drummond Locomotive Society to enable No 30053 to steam through the Purbecks again.
Andrew P. M. Wright

2 December 1989. 'My overriding impression is one of professional teamwork by people who are enjoying their work. The visit reconfirmed my belief that the greatest commercial value to both parties now lies in a steam operation into the 'up' bay platform at Wareham,' he ended.

As the Swanage Railway entered a new decade, 1990 saw its tracks steadily extend still further towards Corfe Castle which was reached during July of that year. Just a few weeks before — and with the dramatic ruins of the Medieval castle coming into view to spur on the volunteers — a tracklaying binge saw the line being extended over half-a-mile in just 10 days.

Volunteers will never forget 1991, though; a year that promised so much but saw a financial crisis that shook the Swanage Railway to its core and took it to within days of extinction. Members were appalled to find that the project had nearly £500,000 worth of liabilities, teetering on the very edge of bankruptcy. The situation was horrendous — a £250,000 loan guarantee secured against railway assets worth more than £1 million from Dorset County Council, owner of much of the railway trackbed; an operating company overdraft of £80,000 and a list of creditors exceeding £120,000.

It was the worst nightmare scenario and one which numbed members thought could never happen. Thanks to the stamina of members, by the end of 1992, £200,000 of debt had been wiped out by prudent budgeting, maximising incomes and sheer hard work.

As the Swanage Railway entered 1993, it was still waiting to hear whether it had cleared its last and most important hurdle; the application for a Light Railway (Extension) Order from the Department of Transport covering the line from Harman's Cross, through Corfe Castle and on to the BR network at Furzebrook. Passenger-carrying trains cannot run without it, despite the fact that the relaid tracks reached Norden — and the site of a small halt and car park just north of Corfe Castle — during the spring of 1992.

Outnumbered by supporters, a small number of objectors in Corfe Castle fired their final desperate salvos during a Public Inquiry by Department of Transport inspector Paul Gane in late May 1992. Those against the Swanage Railway claimed it

Below:

A historic moment on the Swanage Railway as 1880 Midland Railway '1F' 0-6-0T No 41708 becomes the first steam engine to run out of Corfe Castle since the end of passenger steam traction on Sunday 18 June 1967, and the Arab-Israeli war. No 41708 slowly heads out of the Challow Hill cutting through the Purbecks and over newly-laid tracks to collect a track-relaying train. Back in 1967, the final passenger steam working to Swanage was a 12-coach RCTS special with rebuilt 'Battle of Britain' class Bulleid Pacific 34089 *602 Squadron* on the Swanage end and Standard '4' tank No 80146 from Salisbury shed on the Wareham end.
Andrew P. M. Wright

Right:

The sharp end of the Purbeck Line as relaid tracks steadily inch towards a long-awaited connection with the BR network near Furzebrook. With the Medieval ruins of Corfe Castle silhouetted behind — an impressive sight remembered by generations of branch train passengers — volunteers carefully position a 60ft track panel on the cleared trackbed on Thursday 12 March 1992, as the Purbeck Line heads for Norden. Since 1977, volunteers have laid over 3,000 tonnes of track from Swanage — 1,000 rails, 12 ,000 sleepers, over 74,000 bolts and 24,000 track chairs.
Andrew P. M. Wright

Below right:

The site of the new Norden Halt, half a mile north of Corfe Castle and close to the main A351 Wareham to Swanage road, in October 1992. Dwarfed in the distance by the looming East Hill of the Purbecks is the metal 'skew arched' bridge for the old Fayle's narrow gauge ball clay tramway that linked the mines with Eldon's Siding, disused by the early 1960s. Norden's halt and car park is a partnership with Purbeck District Council which — like many other local authorities and official bodies — was sceptical about the success and usefulness of a relaid Swanage branch.
Andrew P. M. Wright

Below:

The way ahead. In the beginning ... there was nothing; the essence of the Swanage Railway's rebuilt Purbeck Line. The trackbed past the old Eldon's ball clay exchange siding (to the right) looking towards Furzebrook on the fine summer afternoon of Sunday 25 August 1991, after volunteers cut back and cleared nearly 20 years of choking undergrowth and full-grown trees! Just days before, walkers couldn't reach this spot even if they wanted to, let alone see anything in front of them — apart from leaves and branches! To the left are the remains of a sleeper-built permanent way hut.
Andrew P. M. Wright

was an unviable toy railway — never of any importance, relevance or benefit to the community; an allegation vociferously denied.

Stronger and wiser, the Swanage Railway is back on target with passenger numbers for 1992 up by 12% to over 100,000 people — despite the economic recession. Santa Special trains were more popular than ever, carrying 9,000 people — equivalent to the population of Swanage — and up 10% on the previous year.

When you travel on the relaid Purbeck Line do not forget that almost everything you see has been 'imported' and rebuilt from nothing; locomotives, coaches, wagons, signalling, rails, sleepers, track chairs — in fact every nut and bolt that goes into making the Swanage Railway.

Volunteers have had to fight long and hard for every inch of ground, for each small step forward, for every triumph. Fast becoming one of Britain's best preserved standard gauge railways, the Purbeck Line has had one of the hardest and longest fights of all — making the rewards sweeter and richer!

Full realisation of the heart-felt dream — a reconnected link with BR and the first passenger train from Swanage to Wareham since January 1972 — may not come to fruition until a quarter of a century since it all began. It has been a long road, with twists and turns no one would dare have predicted; but a journey two generations of volunteers are proud to have made, despite the many disappointments and sad losses along the way; physical, personal and emotional.

A poignant tribute to members past and present, the Swanage Railway is evidence of the strength and resilience of the human spirit against all the odds. Miracles certainly do happen — and Dorset's Purbeck Line is remarkable proof of that.